The Man Behind the Music

"The Legendary Carl Davis"

by

Carl H. Davis, Sr.

The Man Behind the Music
The Legendary Carl Davis

Copyright © 2009 by: Carl H. Davis, Sr.

Printed in the United States

ISBN: 9780983131724

All rights reserved solely by the author. The author certifies all contents are original and do not infringe upon the legal rights of any other person or work. No part of this book may be reproduced in any form without the permission of the publisher. The views expressed in this book are not necessarily those of the publisher.

The accounts depicted in this book are from the author's perspective and reflect the author's best recollection of the subject matter and events and may be completely subjective. Neither the publisher or the author represents that this work reflects all available views, or claims perfect accuracy in all subject matter; but does reflect the author's honest attempt to convey the subject matter according to his perception of the events as he experienced and interpreted them. In conveying the accounts in this book, the author does not represent himself to be a historical authority concerning the subject matter of this book.

Those expressing written acknowledgements for Carl Davis in this book does not constitute an endorsement of any of the books contents, but were submitted independently and separately from the literary content.

Cover design by: Latoya Bady,
                     TBady Graphic Designs
                     Chicago Illinois
                     Tbady@live.com

Literary consultation services provided by: Dennis James Woods

Life To Legacy,LLC
www.Life2legacy.com
P.O. Box 1239
Matteson, IL 60443
(877) 267-7477

Presented to:

To order this book go to:

www.CarlDavisStory.com

To email Carl Davis:

Club54@aol.com

Table of Contents

Acknowledgements	i
Introduction	ii
Chapter 1	1
Chapter 2	20
Chapter 3	35
Chapter 4	47
Chapter 5	67
Chapter 6	80
Chapter 7	92
Chapter 8	104
Chapter 9	112
Chapter 10	119
Chapter 11	129
Chapter 12	144
Chapter 13	160
Chapter 14	167
Letters From My Friends	173
Disc Jockey and Radio Stations List	186
Precious Moments In Time	193

Acknowledgements

I would like to take this opportunity to thank everyone listed below for your love and support over the years. To my family, friends, loved ones, music business associates or contributors to this book, I sincerely thank you from the bottom of my heart. Without your participation in the various aspects of my life, I could not have made it this far, nor would events contained in this book and the wonderful life that I have lived been possible.

This book is dedicated to my wonderful children: Pamela, Brian (1957-2010), Carl II, Tre'c, Julio and Betsy, Kelli and Julian, Carleen and Jaime. I love you all so so much! To my "ma" Florence Gourdine, my mother-in-law who always has my back. Barbara (Elaine) Clark and Patricia Clark my sisters-in-law for making me feel at home in South Carolina. And of course, my precious wife Dedra Gourdine-Davis for hanging in there with me through thick and thin all these years. To the entire Davis family of which there are many nieces, nephews, and grandchildren.

To Bill Dahl for his contributions and diligence in transcribing my story to text and laying the foundation for this book – I am infinitely grateful. To the contributing editor, Dr. Dennis J. Woods, who transformed this work from a diamond in the rough to a literary gem, and his lovely wife Chantia.

To Aundre Miller, for his work re-mastering the CD, and his lovely wife Joyce. To P.J. Willis for his production work on the CD, and to Remell Nichols for all of her assistance.

And finally, to my good friend William (Country) James for just being there. My son Maurice White and of course Gus Redmond, Marianne Eggleston, James Alexander, Eddie and Verleen Thomas, Jack Daniels, Marshall Thompson, Howard Hamlin, Herb Kent, Al and Rita Fry, Garland Floyd, Tom Lewis, Maurice Cobb, Cornelius Dykes, W.L. Lillard and Rick Tabor. I would also like to thank Johnny Collins, John Wilson, Gerri Harris, JoAnne Brooks, Fannie McCullough and Sandra Price. God bless you all!

Introduction

"How in the hell did I end up in this mess?" That nagging thought kept running through my mind like an audio track that keeps looping over and over again. Suddenly, that moment of introspection was abruptly interrupted as the bailiff authoritatively commanded, "All rise." There I stood in this intimidating Newark, New Jersey federal courtroom filled with witnesses, attorneys, and six defendants, of which I was one. An ambitious prosecutorial team, out to prove a point, was headed up by an opportunistic lead prosecutor trying to make a name for himself. They were already smelling blood in the water – all of them like sharks circling their prey before the kill.

It was January, 1976. The blustery winter weather was an uncannily appropriate setting for the chilly climate that had settled in the courtroom as the judge took his seat on the bench. The jury had reached their verdict – it was judgment day. After everyone had settled down, for a moment you could hear a pin drop, and the only thing I could now hear was the sound of my heart pounding increasingly and louder.

There we were, me and six other Brunswick Records executives, all accused of embezzling hundreds of thousands of dollars; allegedly by selling records off the books, thus depriving our recording artists of their hard earned royalties. But that wasn't all. The indictment also accused us of paying disc jockeys and program directors across the country to play our records on the radio, an illegal practice called payola.

Look, I'm not perfect and I'm not claiming to be no saint either. I've lost my temper at times, made some mistakes, had an enemy or two – but this! Not in a million years have I ever stolen anything from the artists that I worked so hard to develop. To what extent my codefendants are guilty, I really can't say. Like me, they must now answer for themselves. All I know is that I'm innocent. But if the jury believed what the prosecutors were saying about my alleged involvement in these crimes, I could be facing prison for a very long time.

Anyone who knew me back home in Chi-town knows I was straight up. I didn't have to steal from anybody and I would never sell out my artists. After all, I was the most successful R&B record producer in Chicago during the 1960s and much of the '70s. I had a string of chart-topping hits, and successful artists like Gene Chandler, the Dells, Major Lance, Walter Jackson,

Jackie Wilson, Tyrone Davis, Barbara Acklin, the Chi-Lites, Young-Holt Unlimited, and plenty more.

When we were on top in Chicago, we made plenty of records that the people wanted to groove to. Business was lucrative because fans didn't mind paying for hit songs and seeing our groups perform live on stage. My formula for success was that I surrounded myself with the best talent out there. The best songwriters, singers, musicians, and producers, they all worked for me. I was a hit maker and innovator, a true record executive extraordinaire. We had a well-oiled machine and a polished product. But my artists were not just product; many of them were also my friends. I loved them, I cared for them, and I nurtured and perfected their talent. I was there for them through the good times as well as the bad times – ask them, and they'll tell you the same thing.

Along the way, I worked with virtually everyone in the rhythm and blues business. My Roladex was fat with contacts and connections. The stars that were idolized at a distance by millions of fans, I knew up close and personal. I could call them all and they would return my phone calls. The deejays, the producers, the record men, they all knew that a call from Carl Davis meant that something good was about to happen and success was soon to follow. My reputation preceded me and I was even respected by the New York and Chicago mobsters who often lurked like dark shadows in the corners of record company boardrooms.

Cassius Clay, I produced a record for him before he changed his name to Muhammad Ali. Louis Armstrong, I worked on a session with him, too. Elton John, I met him in England and convinced him to write me a couple of songs for Walter Jackson, one of my artists. Sam Cooke, Curtis Mayfield, Aretha Franklin, Little Richard, Sammy Davis, Jr., Kenny "Babyface" Edmonds before he went solo – I knew them all and worked with most of them.

But that was then – this is now. Now, here I sit with my life in the hands of twelve jurors, a dozen ominous strangers who are supposed to be a jury of my peers, but who really only know me in the context of these false allegations and trumped up charges. In his closing arguments, the prosecutor has already painted us as racketeers who used our company's accounts to line our pockets with illegal profits. And he carefully instructed the jurors not to be star struck with our accomplishments or our famous associations.

It was so surreal. There I was sitting at the table with Brunswick Records' boss Nat Tarnopol, the man who had brought me into the company, mentored me and made me his partner. Both of us innocent until proven guilty, anxiously waiting for the jury foreman to read the verdict. Were the charges really true about my co-defendants? I had no way of knowing. The only thing that I was sure of was that I had been accused of crimes I did not commit. As I sat there caught up in a seemingly endless moment, there was little time to reflect on how I ended up neck deep in these choppy legal waters.

To the casual observer in the courtroom, I may have seemed calm, cool and collected. However, beneath the thin veneer of confidence I am inconspicuously desperate. Therefore, in my mind, in an instant of time, I retreat to a period and place far away from this legal dilemma that would determine my fate.

Chapter 1

Humble Beginnings

    I was born September 19, 1934 on the Southside of Chicago, and as it turned out, a lot of crazy stuff was going down in America that year. The Great Depression was in full swing, while gangsters like John Dillinger and Bonnie and Clyde terrorized the banking establishments and law enforcement agencies in a multi-state crime spree of bank robberies and murder. However, during that fateful year of 1934, John Dillinger was gunned down by Melvin Purvis outside of Chicago's Biograph Theatre, just a couple of miles north of the neighborhood where I was born. In the same year, Bonnie and Clyde were gunned down in Bienville Parish, Louisiana, just a couple hundred miles from where my parents were raised.

    However, on a much lighter note, in 1934 a performing arts venue opened its doors and would become the gateway to national and international fame for countless black entertainers who were fortunate enough to grace its stage – the Apollo Theatre. The Apollo would be a place that I would become very familiar with years later as a producer and record label executive.

The Man Behind the Music

By today's standards, we had a large family, although families with ten or more children were not all that uncommon back in those days. I was the eleventh child of my father William Adam Davis and my mother Mattie. My father came up the hard way, and was raised during very tough times. He was born and raised in St. James Parish, Louisiana. The Ku Klux Klan was running rampant, economic times were very tight, and there was little money to be made by black people with little education. Though he wasn't a highly educated intellect, my daddy made it because he was an expert survivor. William Davis was a tough no-nonsense man with a reputation of being someone you didn't want to rub the wrong way. He was not the one to play games with, and he didn't take no mess from anyone, black or white.

On the other hand, my mother Mattie Gibson was raised in Donaldsonville, Louisiana. Her upbringing was different from my father's. She was raised amongst a musically inclined family, where she learned to sing. She used to sing in establishments around town with her brothers, who had formed a local band. A couple of the Gibson brothers were also fortunate enough to get jobs as Pullman Porters, working the passenger train routes throughout the North and the South. Back then, this was a choice job for a black man to have. My mom's brothers could have passed for white because their mother was Caucasian, but this was an advantage they chose not to exploit. However, their fair complexion and straight hair opened many doors for them that may not have been opened for darker skinned blacks with more ethnic features. The combination of talent and good looks fared well for the Gibsons and their musical endeavors.

Since a lot of their band's engagements were church affairs, they would sing traditional hymns and church songs in those venues. However, when they sang in secular establishments, they would jazz it up a bit and perform material from Lena Horne and other popular entertainers of that era.

As the band's popularity and number of engagements increased, they needed a roadie who could help the band with setting up equipment and who could also double as a bodyguard to look after their prized lead singer – my mother Mattie. So they hired someone who was perfect for the job – my dad – and that's how my mother and father met. After working with the band for a while, it became obvious that there was a little more going on with William than moving equipment around stage. A mutual attraction had developed between Mattie and William that evolved into a romantic relationship, and soon they fell in love and got married. As fate would have it, there could not have been a better bodyguard than someone who would vow to love, cherish and protect my mother till death do them part.

It's amazing how situations that we encounter can become pivotal events that change the course of our lives. Prior to my family's migration up north to Chicago, my parents already had four children; my brothers Herman, William, and Arlington, and my sister Barbara. They were all born in Louisiana. But because of some extenuating circumstances, Chicago became an option of necessity when my father faced the possibility of swinging from the end of a rope.

Like I said earlier, my daddy didn't take nothing from anyone, black or white. It all started when a white man who happened to like my father offered him a job as a saw man at the local sawmill. Daddy quickly gained the respect of his boss because he was the best worker they had. One day after a long shift at the mill, daddy came home from work and walked into a situation that he could not have anticipated. Something was wrong; something was really wrong. When he walked into the house, my mother's normal jovial spirit was dampened by the stream of tears that rolled down her face. Immediately he asked her what was wrong? Mama, being the sweet peaceful type, didn't want to tell him because she knew what was going to happen when she did. But after daddy insisted, she finally told him that a white man took inappropriate flirtatious liberties with her and called her degrading names while she was in town at the store. Being the good Christian woman that she was, she tried to leave the store, but he just kept on disrespecting her and calling her names. When daddy heard this, he snapped.

You see, you have to understand the times in which they lived. It was the deep South, in the early 1920s. In those days, a black man couldn't even look a white man in the eye, let alone talk back to him, without the fear of being lynched. But my daddy didn't care about any of that. Nobody, and I mean nobody, disrespected his wife without getting their ass whipped. This white man was no exception to that rule. My dad went back into town, caught up with this fool, and beat him silly, breaking his jaw and everything.

When word about what my dad did spread around town, the whites were outraged and there was talk about lynching my father. The dust had hardly settled when one night, daddy heard someone outside on the porch.

The Man Behind the Music

When he opened the door, it was a white man, but it wasn't a Klan member. To his surprise, it was his boss from the sawmill standing there holding a shotgun and saying that he would shoot anyone coming to lynch my daddy. He told my dad that there wasn't much time left, but that he'd stand guard while we packed up to get out of town. Although daddy was rough and tough and could stand against the best of them, daddy wasn't anybody's fool either. He knew his days were numbered if he stayed in Louisiana. And chances were, they wouldn't just come after him, because angry lynch mobs have been known to wipe out whole families. So my mom, dad, brothers, and sister packed up what belongings they could in a hurry. They all got in the back of the boss's pickup truck and sped away to the train station. Once there, his boss paid for their one-way tickets to Chicago.

Before daddy got on the train, his boss informed him that he'd called ahead to contacts at the main Post Office in Chicago and lined up a janitor's position for him. These acts of benevolence and bravery accentuated the fact that there are good and bad people in every race. Daddy was grateful, and thanked him for everything that he did for his family. They shook hands and said their goodbyes. Daddy was the last of the family to get on the train, and after he did, he never looked back. Having escaped with their lives from treachery that lurked in the backwoods and bayous of south Louisiana, they faced a new way of life up North in the sprawling urban jungle of Chicago, Illinois.

Getting acclimated to life in the big city must have agreed with my parents very well, because in the years to follow, they had seven more children. Born in Chicago were Edward, Clifford, Fred, Helen, Kenneth, George, and me. We lived in an apartment building at 48th and Champlain on the Southside. When my mother went into labor with me, there was no time to make it to Michael Reese or Cook County Hospital, so I was born right there in our second floor apartment – a fact that I would hear occasionally as my older siblings teased me about it.

My childhood was full of fond memories of being raised on Chicago's Southside. I loved my neighborhood and all my friends. Our apartment building was cool, too. All of the apartments had alley-side windows that you could climb out of and stand on the fire escapes. From there, the older boys, who were real fire escape daredevils, would leap over to the fire escape ladder and ride it down to the alley below. Man, it looked like so much fun and it looked so easy to do. Just jump, grab and ride it down – it's easy. My brothers were the only ones who did all the acrobatics for the longest time, up until I got the courage to try it myself. One day I got up there when my brothers were hanging out in the alley. They looked up and saw me about to jump.

They yelled, "No Carl, don't do it!"

But I didn't listen. Instead, I jumped. Well, I managed to jump far enough to grab hold of the fire escape, but my momentum proved to be too much for my young hands to handle, and I lost my grip and fell. We were living on the second floor, so that meant I fell from the second floor all the way down to the basement. Fortunately, there were some old tires down there, and I landed on them, so I didn't kill myself. Besides the bruise that I received on my behind, I also received another one on my young ego. However, I learned a valuable lesson about the perils of mimicking my older brothers. Having a big boy's imagination in a little boy's body proved to be quite a contradiction, and a painful lesson learned the hard way.

During the time that I was raised, there were a lot of families from the South migrating to northern cities like Chicago. The prospects for employment were much better, therefore, communities like ours were growing as families moved in seeking to make a better life for themselves. However, most of us were poor, and the area on Chicago's Southside where we lived was considered the ghetto. But of course, words like the ghetto are not in a child's typical vocabulary. To me, it was a nice neighborhood. We were right off the alley, where we would often play. I had plenty of friends. To us, it was just where we lived. We had no socio-economic preconceptions. Most of us kids were insulated from knowing our family's economic status anyway. All we cared about was where to play and who to play with.

Indeed, the times were different in comparison to today's hi-tech modern society. There were wholesome things, like the watermelon men who used to come by on the horse-drawn wagons with a load of watermelons that they sold off the back. I still remember the clunky sounds the horse's shoes would make as they proceeded up the cobblestone alleys. As a matter of fact, one of my first jobs was selling those watermelons. I remember it like it was yesterday. People would hang out of the window and yell down, "Send me up a watermelon! How much are they?" Then I would grab one of those juicy watermelons, throw it over my shoulders, and run it up to them. Occasionally, I'd even get a tip. I made a few dollars doing that and enjoyed it, because I'd liked the feeling of having money in my pockets, especially when I went to school.

During the week, my mother used to send us to school sharp as a tack. I'd have on starched khaki pants and a clean, freshly ironed matching shirt. To look at me, you would have never known we were poor, and my mother wouldn't have had it any other way. Everybody knew that the Davis kids were all well kept kids.

We were also a real community back in those days. Everybody knew everybody else. If you were getting into mischief in the neighborhood and the neighbors saw you, they'd whip your butt first, and then they would call your mom and dad, and you'd get another whipping when you got home. Everybody was caring about everybody, and the concept of a village raising a child was in full application. But seeing how it is now, I can truly say that those were the good old days.

By the time I was seven, my older brothers and sisters had left the home to start their own families, so eventually we moved to a wood frame house at 711 E. 69th Street in the Englewood neighborhood. It was on the Southside, near the corner of 69th and Langley. There, we had a wood-burning stove for heat. Other homes used coal or heating oil. But not our house. My dad had to chop the wood to keep a fire going for heat.

A unique aspect about this house was that there was a huge vacant lot next door, where my mom planted corn, tomatoes, potatoes, beets, and anything else that could grow from the soil. Back in those days, they used to call them victory gardens. It covered the entire yard, from front to back. Every year, we'd have to dig up this yard so mama could plant. By that time, it was down to my brothers Fred, Kenneth, George, and me. Clifford still lived there, but he was away in the Navy. We were all the siblings left at the house, so we were my mom's garden workers. All of us were out there, tilling and turning dirt, pulling weeds and chucking rocks, just so we could have fresh vegetables on our dinner table. It was hard work. Eventually, mama even planted an apple and orange tree back there in her victory garden. Thank goodness we lived in the city because knowing my mom, we probably would have been raising some cows, hogs, chickens, and everything else, too.

One of the many fond memories that I have of my childhood is the

Carl H. Davis, Sr.

day that I met my first celebrity. One Saturday morning, my dad and I were walking down Cottage Grove, heading towards the Pershing Ballroom, when we passed by a very popular barbershop. Right as we were passing the entrance, who should walk out but none other than the Brown Bomber himself, Joe Louis? I couldn't believe my eyes. Not only was Joe Louis a champion heavyweight boxer, but he was a legend and hero in the African American community. To see a black man who was famous and had an impeccable reputation back in the days where you didn't see a lot of respected blacks in the media, was a really big thing.

My father walked up to him and respectfully acknowledged him by simply saying, "Joe Louis." Smiling as he shook his hand, my father did something that I will never forget. My father said, "Mr. Louis, I would like you to shake my boy's hand, too." Joe Louis smiled, looked down at me, and extended his huge right hand towards me. As I reached up to shake his hand, I stood there with my mouth gaping wide open, looking up at this giant of a man. Ironically, the same right hand that knocked out countless opponents gently engaged my tender young hand in a friendly handshake. Wow – I was too through. As long as I live, I will never forget that day, the day I stood between two giants – one my personal hero and the other a legend – my daddy and Joe Louis.

During that time, I was attending McCosh Elementary School at 6525 S. Champlain. Then each day after school, I also went to Catholic lessons at a nearby Catholic School. My brother George, who is a year-and-a-half older than me, was my best friend then and still is now. However, George and I were different. George was the good kid who did all the right things, while I was a problem child who liked getting into mischief. George was the way every kid should be. He always did his homework and studied hard, and he never gave the teachers a hard time. And since George was a model student, they even made him a crossing guard. For a grammar school kid back in those days, that was real respect.

George used to be so proud of wearing that white crossing guard belt. It was a real badge of honor. You had to really be an upstanding and responsible student to be allowed that position. Before and after school, George would be on various corners like a soldier guarding his post. Oftentimes, I would pass by him and make a funny face to get his attention, but he always stayed focused on the job at hand. He would walk out in the middle of the street, and with one hand extended, he held up traffic, while with the other hand he beckoned the kids to hurry across the street. Even as a kid, George took his responsibilities seriously. He also got a job at the local grocery store working in the afternoons and evenings. The worst thing I could ever recall him doing was, while he was working at the store, he'd sneak us Twinkies and candy through the back door. He didn't mind that so much because I'd save him some for when he got home.

But as for me, I was the flipside of the coin. I wasn't a model student. I didn't like doing homework and I certainly wasn't interested in being no crossing guard. What I liked to do was fight. And if I didn't like you, chances were that if we crossed paths enough, we were going to go at it.

As I grew older, I started ditching school. I would even go downtown to my dad's job at the main Post Office and tell him that I was with my class over at the museum and I needed lunch money. My dad would be in a real good mood while his co-workers were around. He'd love showing off in front of his friends, saying, "This is my youngest boy Carl. Whatcha need, son?" He'd go in his pocket, rumble out two or three dollars in change, and give it to me. I'd be just as happy as a lark, running straight to a movie or the store, and spending that money.

Living right across the street from McCosh Elementary was a lovely young lady named Theresa Fambro. I had a serious childhood crush on her and tried my best to court her. Even though she treated me nicely, she wanted nothing to do with me because by then, I already had a reputation for being a young troublemaker. As it turned out, Theresa went on to become a columnist for the Defender, Chicago's premier African-American newspaper. And another very close lifelong friend who also worked at the Defender, was Earl Callaway.

During that time, two of my best friends were a couple of neighborhood kids named Arthur Logan and Jimmy Jones. Arthur was the smart one, Jimmy was the devilish one, and I was somewhere in the middle. Put the three of us together and it wouldn't be long before we'd get some trouble brewing. Stuff like throwing eggs at windows wasn't our cup of tea. We had more sophisticated devilment in mind.

For example, back in those days people rode the trolley cars as a primary means of transportation. Trolley cars were similar to trains in that they rode on tracks. However, their power source came from overhead electrical wires that ran above the streets on the trolley route. The trolley cars had two poles that extended up above the car and connected with the power lines above to get the electrical current to move the trolley cars. There were also two connector wires located on the back of the trolley. If you pulled out those connector wires, the trolley cars would stop dead in their tracks.

Sixty-Seventh Street was one of the busiest trolley routes on the Southside, passing right through our neighborhood. The thought of making one of those trolley cars stop in the middle of the street was too much for our mischievous minds to pass up. So we would run behind those trolleys and pull those connector wires loose, and sure enough, the trolley would immediately lose power and stop. We would then scurry on our way, laughing up a storm. The trolley driver would be pissed off and cursing because he'd have to get out and fix the wires. The passengers would be ticked off because they'd be stuck on a disabled trolley car. And don't mention the traffic delays. But to us, this was all in a day's fun.

Unfortunately, youthful pranks of this nature were not enough to keep my rambunctious buddies amused. One day, Jimmy broke into the office of a used car lot and stole several sets of cars keys. But that was not all. He searched through the office until he found a checkbook full of blank personal checks. In the checkbook were some canceled checks that had the lot owner's signature on them. Jimmy studied the signature, made a few practice runs, and then forged several checks made out to myself, Arthur, and others in our crew. He gave car keys to different people around the neighborhood, who ended up driving off with cars from this used car lot. My brother Kenneth got a car, and he didn't even know how to drive yet.

Like the silly kids we were, we thought nothing of the consequences of our foolish actions. We cashed the checks, spending the money on junk food and gym shoes. Within the space of just a few days, we graduated from disabling trolley cars to cashing forged checks and grand theft auto.

A few days after this indiscretion, we were playing handball at the McCosh Elementary playground when suddenly three police cars pulled up, lights flashing and sirens blaring. We were surrounded so quickly that our heads were spinning. They exited their squad cars and came over to us asking, "Which one of you is Jimmy Jones?" So Jimmy looked around and sheepishly raised his hand. "You're coming with us!" Then they asked, "Who's Arthur Logan?" Arthur raised his hand. "You're going with us too!"

Then they named a couple of other guys, but they didn't call me. Right at that moment, I was thinking that I was the lucky one who was about to get away. But my wishful thinking was shattered when they said, "Take 'em all down! We'll get all this hashed out at the station!" Now, I was terrified because I still had one of those checks in my back pocket.

They crammed us all into the back of one squad car for a very uncomfortable ride down to the police station at 63rd and Dorchester. I seized on this small window of opportunity to solicit the help of the kid upon whose lap I was sitting. Desperately, I told him to reach into my back pocket, get that check out, and shove it down in the back seat cushion. So he did. After we arrived at the station, the interrogation started. They wanted to know who was forging these checks, and what happened to these cars. Even though they tried their best to intimidate me, I wasn't about to give up my buddies. So eventually, they let everybody go but me and Jimmy. I ended up going to the juvenile detention home.

Finally, we went to court for a preliminary hearing. They marched me, Jimmy, and the rest of the youth who had trial that day into the courtroom. They sat us all in the jury booth, as we waited for our case to be called. I looked out into the courtroom and saw my dad sitting over by the witnesses. I was scared to death, because my daddy didn't look very happy at all. Then all of a sudden, the guy who owned the lot came over there and started harassing us: "Give me back my keys. Where's my checkbook?" That's when my dad got up and confronted this man asking,

"Excuse me, are you a police officer?"

He said, "No, I'm the one that they stole the stuff from!"

So he told him, "Well, you get the hell away from my kid!"

He told me, "Don't you say another damn word to him! Wait for the judge."

Soon the judge came into the courtroom, and the bench trial started. That's when my father got up, and he said,

"Your honor, I would like to speak."

The judge said, "Proceed, Mr. Davis. Go right ahead."

He said, "Your Honor, I have eleven kids at home – nine boys and two girls. And ain't none of my kids been in no trouble with the law, cause I teach 'em better than that. Carl is the first one that ever went astray, so if you'll just send him home with me this time, I promise you you'll never see him again. That's all I got to say."

The judge contemplated what my father said and responded,

"You know, Mr. Davis, since you've done such a great job on those ten you mentioned, why don't you stick with them, but this one, we're gonna keep for a while."

Believe it or not, I was glad when the judge said no, because I knew my father was going to kill me. Then the judge slammed down his gavel and said,

"Ninety days in the Audy Home."

I was only twelve or thirteen at time, and that three-month sentence sounded like years. Ironically, little did I know at the time that this wouldn't be my last time in a court being accused of stealing.

The Audy Home was located out on Foster Avenue on the city's far Northwest Side. It was like a college campus. There wasn't any barbed wire; just a wrought iron fence was all that was between us and the surrounding community. We lived in cottages. Each cottage housed fifteen to twenty kids. There must have been ten cottages on the grounds.

When I got there, I had to make like I was a tough guy. There was an older guy who was what they called a cottage captain, who was supposedly in charge of us. He was an inmate as well, but had been there for a longer time. This young Irish or Italian kid was in charge of assigning our chores, like cleaning up or taking out the garbage, but he was getting on my nerves. One day during recreation, we were out playing basketball. He just kept getting in my face. If I got the ball, there he was. If I tried to shoot, there he was, in my face and talking trash. Enough was enough. I took the basketball and hit him in the head with it. So we started going at it. He knocked my glasses off. And I grabbed hold of his hair and wouldn't let go. Neither one of us got the best of each other, so when it was all over, we were alright with each other and he appointed me to be assistant cottage captain.

As the weeks progressed, I found out that my friend Jimmy Jones, who actually did all the stealing, was in a cottage next door, and they were giving him a hard time. When we played that cottage in a softball game, I asked Jimmy, "Who is the guy giving you all this trouble?" He pointed the guy out. I went over there with a bat, and I told him who I was. I said, "My brother Jimmy tells me you're giving him a hard time. Next time I hear about you giving him a hard time about anything, I'm gonna take this bat and knock your block off!" It worked. Jimmy didn't have any more problems with this guy until we left.

I was only in the Audy Home for about three months, but by that time, my family had moved from 69th Street to 44th and Drexel in a basement apartment. There were still some white people living over there, and racial tensions were high. One day I was walking down Drexel Avenue heading to the store, when a few white boys tried to jump me. But there were two things that I could do well: fight and run. I got in a few good licks on a couple of them, and then I broke for it. In general, us black kids were better fighters, but every now and then, you would catch one of those white boys who was a real scrapper and who would go toe-to-toe with you. We had some pretty good fights while I lived in that neighborhood.

After becoming more acclimated with our new neighborhood, I ran into some guys I knew who lived over by 44th and Cottage Grove. One of their names was Jardine. Back then, the west side of Cottage Grove was predominantly black, with mostly white on the east side of Cottage. One day we all got together, and they accepted me into their little clique. We rode our bicycles to an area around 46th and Forrestville, into some alley, and they handed out guns. They gave me a gun, too. We then went into this garage where they were running a policy operation, also known as numbers. People would come in there, and they would play certain numbers. If they won, they would go right back to the place where they played the number and pick up their winnings. That's the place we stuck up. I was so scared, I didn't know what I was doing. I was only about fourteen or so, but all I remember was that I had a gun in my hand and was shaking like a leaf. My nervousness was so noticeable that the policy guy, who had both hands raised, insisted, "Quit shaking! You're gonna mess around and shoot somebody!" It was obvious that I was more afraid of him than he was of me, but with one major difference – I was the one with the gun.

After we robbed them, we got away with approximately one hundred dollars. So we ran out of that garage and sped away on our bikes. After that, I never hung around with those guys anymore. These young thugs were way over my head because they were serious criminals heading for the penitentiary or the grave. Fortunately, we were never caught. All these numbers rackets were run by gangsters who'd track you down and beat you down. But I got away with it. Not too long after that incident, our family moved again and I was grateful because I didn't like the neighborhood anyway.

After doing time in the Audy Home, the public school system didn't want me back in regular school, but they wanted me to attend reform school. My only option was to attend one of the parochial schools in the area, which was a Seven Day Adventist School on Oakwood Boulevard, right off of Lake Shore Drive on 39th Street. They enrolled me there. It was called Shiloh Christian Academy. They had this principal who was a strict disciplinarian. If you got out of line, they would take you down to the basement and make you pull down your pants and bend over a chair. They had this big old wooden paddle, and would proceed to tearing your butt up. Depending on what you did and how mad you made the teacher, that's what determined how many swats you'd get. Getting hit with that thing ten times was torture. This kind of corporal punishment helped me stay on the straight and narrow, and as a result, I ended up graduating from Shiloh Christian Academy.

After the perils of my grammar school years, finally I enrolled at Englewood High School. One of the highlights of being at Englewood was that I made the football team. I was number 46. Back then, you played both offense and defense. So I was a running back on offense, and I was a cornerback on defense. At one point during our season, one of my teammates who played safety was injured. So they asked me to play that position as well. In one hotly contested game, there I was playing safety, but I got my roles crossed up. Normally, at cornerback, the first guy who comes by, you let him go by and you focus on the second one. The problem was that I was thinking like a cornerback in a safety's position. All of a sudden, this guy runs by me, and I just let him go. Then, their quarterback threw a bomb to this receiver who had just blazed right past me. It was like it was in slow motion. I saw the ball in the air, and I thought, "Oh, no!" The coaches were having a fit and screaming at the top of their lungs, "Carl, get him. Get back there!" But it was too late. I could not have possibly caught up with him by that point. Fortunately, he was no better at his position than I was at mine, and he dropped the pass.

The football field wasn't the only place where I was challenged at Englewood. I was struggling in my academics, and I was particularly horrible in math. I had a math teacher named Miss Levin, and she wouldn't cut me any slack, football team or not. If you failed a class, you were automatically off the team. To me, playing football was my whole reason for going to school, so when I flunked math, I ended up dropping out of high school altogether. However, later on, I earned my GED.

After dropping out, I didn't know what to do with myself, but I knew I had to do something quick. So I joined the Air Force, even though I was only sixteen years old. I fudged my age by using my brother Kenneth's birth date, which was April 4, 1931, and then forging some baptismal records by switching our names on the certificate. That's how I was able to join the Air Force in 1951, when I was still too young.

Ironically, I actually attempted to join the Air Force once before, but was unsuccessful because there was a problem with my name, not my age. My full name is Carl Henry Davis. My mother named me Carl Henry after a bald-headed comic strip character from the Herald American newspaper. At the time, my brother George wanted to go into the Air Force, and I tried to enlist with him. In order for anyone to enlist, you had to bring your birth certificate. So I went down to the department of statistics, and there was no record of a Carl Davis having been born on September 19, 1934. Being obviously disturbed by this revelation, I came home and told my mother what had happened. That's when my mother said, "Look under Adams." She explained that right before I was born, my father was between jobs and was applying for some kind of welfare benefit. Some of his friends had told him, "Whatever you do, make sure you put the right name down, because without the right name, you may not get your welfare check." So he was entered on my birth certificate under his real name, which was William Adams. When I heard that, I was blown away.

For the first time in my life, I found out the devastating news that my father's name was not his real name, and that I was born Carl Adams, not Carl Henry Davis. I went back down to the department of statistics, and sure enough, my name was down there as Carl Adams. At that point, I wasn't sure about anything, and I thought, "Maybe I'm adopted!" Everybody else in the family was named Davis, except me. When I came back home, my mother explained everything. She said, "Your dad's mother and father got divorced. So she remarried a guy named Davis. Instead of making it legal, your dad just thought he'd use the name Davis. So from that point on, your father used the last name Davis." That's how all my brothers and sisters were named Davis, when historically my father's name was actually Adams.

To avoid any legal pitfalls later on, I had my lawyer legally change my name. I took out Henry and just put Carl H. Davis. But I had to go back to McCosh Elementary and the church because they both had my name down as just Carl Davis. To this day, I'm the only child out of the eleven of us that ever carried my father's real last name, Adams.

After enlisting in the Air Force, I was stationed at Sampson Air Force Base in Geneva, New York for basic training. While at basic, all of us were given a series of aptitude tests to determine what job we were qualified for. My test results indicated that I was best suited to be a clerk-typist. I had no idea what that was, and it didn't sound appealing to me, either. After basic training, I was transferred to Cheyenne, Wyoming, where I went through training to be a clerk. While there, I befriended a young man named Orville Pitts, who was a very talented boxer. He and I ran around together and had some really good times. Years later, he went on to professional boxing and even fought Joey Maxin, the light heavyweight champion, in a bout that he unfortunately lost on points; but I'll always remember him as being a winner and a friend.

After completing my clerk-typist training, I was transferred to Barksdale Air Force Base in Shreveport, Louisiana. Ironically, the same state that my family had to flee from for fear of being lynched, would be the same state that I would be stationed at during my first tour of duty outside of training. Maybe it was in my blood from my father and mother's past, but me and Louisiana did not get along. Being born and raised in Chicago, I didn't know anything about the level of prejudice and racism that you found in the deep south.

In Chicago, I had some skirmishes with white kids, particularly in my old neighborhood that was close to the dividing line between the black and white communities. Cottage Grove was that dividing line. If you were on the east side of the street where the cemetery was, you were going to run into some white kids, and you were going to get into a fight. But I really loved that neighborhood.

While you were on the airbase, nobody was supposed to be overtly prejudice. But off the base, out in town, that was a completely different story. During that time, many of the whites wanted blacks to always be subservient. They expected you to say, "Yes, ma'am," or "No, ma'am," that kind of thing. Well, I was a Chicagoan, and the furthest south I had ever been up until that point was the Southside of Chicago. I wasn't about to do all that and I didn't do all that. My stubborn demeanor baffled many of the town folks and some would even ask the rhetorical question, "You're not from down here, are you?" And I would say, "That's right!"

Barksdale Airbase had a curfew. If you didn't get back before a certain time, you couldn't get back on the base. So you had to stay out in town overnight, and get back to the base first thing in the morning before they would declare you AWOL. If you did have to stay in town overnight, there were no hotels – they had boarding houses. If you had a girl and you wanted to take care of some business, you'd go to one of those little boarding houses and rent a room.

One night, me and one of my fellow airmen were running down the street trying to catch the bus to go back to the base. There was a police car parked right on the corner, and as we were passing by, the officer stuck his head out the window and said, "It's a nice day, ain't it boys?" I responded in my typical nonconformist manner, "That's right," and I kept on running. Apparently, that was the wrong response. He darted out in front of us and cut us off, and he said, "Boys, let's do this again. I want you to go back down yonder to that corner, and I'm gon' let you run by me again. I'm gonna ask you the same question one more time. If you don't give me the right answer, I'm gonna take your head and put it in the window, and roll the window up on your neck. Then I'm going to wear your asses out with this here Billy club!"

The guy with me was from the South. He said, "Carl, what's wrong with you man? You ain't in Chicago. Missing the bus won't be our only problem if you start mess'n round with the police down here!" I suddenly had a change of heart. So just like the good airmen we were, we went back to the same spot and we trotted on back by the policeman again. He stuck his head out the window and said, "Nice morning, ain't it boys?" I said, "Yes, sir!" I kept running, jumped on the bus, and went back to the base. That really hurt me to have to do that, but I'm glad my experience turned out to be one where only my feelings were hurt. As most of us know, just a few years later in Mississippi, Emmett Till, another young black kid from Chicago's Southside, would be brutally murdered for supposedly saying the wrong thing to a white woman.

While stationed at Barksdale, I was assigned to the supply detachment, working in the orderly room, which was the administrative part of the

Carl H. Davis, Sr.

supply operation. My job was the official gofer (go for this and go for that). Whenever a phone call would come in for me, the civilian ladies would holler out, "Carl, pick up!" And I'd go pick it up. This is how it was all day long, day in day out. However, there was one occasion when the phone rang and I happened to answer it. The call was for a white lady named Virginia. So I hollered out, "Virginia, pick up!" When she heard this, she turned as red as a Washington apple and said,

"What did you call me?"

I replied in a slightly perturbed manner, "Your name! Your name's Virginia right?"

She said, "You don't call me that, you stupid nigger! You call me, Miss Virginia, or Missus. You ain't got no right to ever address me by my first name!"

Now I'm really upset, and I angrily responded, "Wait a minute. I'm in the Air Force. I don't have to put up with this crap."

The white folks were having a conniption. So they rushed to get the officer who was in charge, because there was no way they were going to tolerate a renegade negro in their midst. The officer immediately comes out to confront me, and he gets all up in my face. Close enough for me to smell his foul breath and feel the heat of his searing bigotry. He angrily exclaimed:

"What are you doing, calling her by her first name? Nigger, you don't know where you are, do you?"

He then reared back like he was about to slap me, and that's when my Southside boxing skills took over. The next thing I knew, I hit that officer so hard that he fell back and busted through the set of swinging doors there in our office. It was just like in the cowboy movies where someone is thrown out of a saloon and bursts through the swinging doors. But this was no Hollywood movie set, and I was no actor; and he certainly was no stunt man. He went flying through those doors and landed flat on his back. He hit the floor hard, as those doors continued to swing back and forth.

I must admit that it felt good when I hit him, but that suddenly gave way to, "Oh my God. What in the world did I just do?" I knew I was in trouble, so I hightailed it out of there and ran all the way back to my headquarters as fast as I could. I immediately reported this incident to my lieutenant, a northerner from New York. I told him exactly what happened and what I did. He was outraged and said that they should not have called me nigger.

The Man Behind the Music

Not a good ten minutes had elapsed before they came. It was like a posse after some bad guys – military police and all. They came running in after me, talking about locking me up. So my lieutenant told the officer that I decked,

"If you press charges against Airman Davis, I'm going to press charges against you because you had no right calling him that. You can't let civilians say that to an airman, either."

So they worked it out between the two of them. I was a corporal at the time of this incident, and they busted me down to a Private First Class. I was very fortunate that I didn't get a court martial, because an enlisted man striking a commissioned officer is a very serious offense that could get you jail time in Leavenworth.

After that incident, my commanding officer felt that I should leave Louisiana – an oddly similar situation that my father found himself facing years before I was born. Soon, the Air Force cut me some new orders and sent me to school to learn how to operate the DSJ Composomatic, a machine that was a predecessor to word processors and computers. And lo and behold, I was good at working this machine. I saved our government lots of money by condensing what was on an 8 ½" by 11" page down to 3" by 5" size with the same message on it. I earned commendations from the command, and I got so good at operating the machine that they put me in charge of it.

But I made a mistake. I took some leave, went back to Chicago during the Christmas holidays, and married my high school sweetheart. After moving back to Shreveport, there were no homes available for us, so I rented a room at a lady's house. What I didn't know was that when I would go to work, my wife would be playing behind my back. She would be at the local tavern dancing and showing her butt. Men were all over her. On one occasion, I received a call from one of my fellow airmen who saw my wife at the tavern. He said, "Man, you'd better get down here, because your wife is acting a fool!" So I went down there, and sure enough, I caught her. I don't know what all she had been doing, but I snatched her out of there and took her back home. Then I told her that she had to go back to Chicago, and I sent her back there. I was terribly humiliated by this whole ordeal and so I requested a transfer for overseas duty. They sent me over to Okinawa for a year or two.

Carl H. Davis, Sr.

While I was stationed in Okinawa, I received some mail from Arthur Logan, one of the guys I'd gotten in trouble with years earlier. Arthur was working for UPS at the time. In the letter, he stated that one day while delivering a package around 46th and Lake Park, my wife answered the door – she was living with another man. I was so ticked off that I wrote him back and chewed him out for telling me this. Clearly, my anger was misplaced. He didn't do anything wrong. He actually did the right thing by telling me the truth.

When I returned from Okinawa, I filed for divorce, which turned out to be a real mess. Oddly enough, my wife didn't want to get divorced. She came over to my parents' house, where I was staying, and wanted to spend the night there with me to try to mend our marriage. The next thing I know, the doorbell rings, and the guy that she had been living with came down there looking for her. He was a grown man in his mid to late twenties. I was still only seventeen years old. But that didn't make any difference to me. I told him, "I don't care who you are. This is my house. You get the hell out of here!"

Then my dad jumped up with a hammer in his hand and threatened to knock his head off. This guy certainly didn't want any part of my dad, so he hurried up and got out of there. That was the last straw with my wife, so I told her to get out. Not long after that, we finally got divorced. Ironically, she and that guy ended up getting married. Good. Those two deserved one another. I was just glad she was out of my life.

In 1954, I was discharged early from the Air Force, after my father got sick and died from cirrhosis of the liver. Though my father was a great man and I loved him dearly, he was an alcoholic and drank himself to death. After he died, the Air Force gave me a General Discharge, under what they called honorable conditions, so I could look after my mom. And since I was my mother's youngest child, this also contributed to their decision to discharge me early. I spent three years in the Air Force, and I didn't particularly care for it. However, I didn't realize at the time that a skill that I learned while in the service would contribute to my career in the music business. As for my brother, the one I followed to the Air Force, he loved it, and made a career out of it, retiring after twenty years of service. After his career in the Air Force, he came to work for me in the music business.

Chapter 2

Nineteen fifty-four turned out to be a year of many major transitions in my life. I was discharged from the Air Force and my father died. But it was also in 1954 that my sister Helen introduced me to June Allison (not the actor). June was a beautiful and very intelligent young lady who attended the same church as my sister. Both my sister and June were cut from the same type of cloth. Both of them were upstanding, nice, clean women. Helen knew that I was recently divorced, but was confident that I would make the right woman a good husband. She told June that she had a brother who just got out of the Air Force, and that she thought the both of us would really hit it off. After talking me up so, she peaked June's interest and arranged for both of us to meet. Sure enough, my sister was right. It was love at first sight. I fell head over heels for Ms. June Allison and we got married later in 1954.

Soon after we were married, we moved into an apartment on 53rd Street right off of Maryland. We had two children together: Pamela June, who was born in June of '55, and Brian Fred, who was born in July of '57. Not having a steady job at the time, we had to leave our apartment and move

Carl H. Davis, Sr.

in with June's foster mother. June's foster mother was really well off, and owned a very nice home located on a corner lot at 77th and Rhodes. Unfortunately, June never knew her real parents, but was raised by her foster mother.

After getting settled, I was able to find odd jobs in and around Chicago during this period. I worked for Argo Starch. I worked for the U.S. Postal Service at Christmas time, and at a Standard gas station that was situated right across the street from my old Seventh Day Adventist school. I worked there for about a year. I then decided that if I was going to get any meaningful employment, I would have to get some more education. Therefore, I used my G.I. benefits and enrolled at Cortez-Peters Business College on 55th Street, located right along where the "L" trains run. I attended there for two years and received my associate's degree in higher accounting and business administration. With a business degree under my belt, coupled with a few years of military training, I felt that I finally had a good shot at landing a job that paid well enough to support my family.

My first break came when I landed a sales position promoting the latest hits handled by Ernie Leaner's United Distributors, which specialized in R&B and blues record labels. I knew right away that this was up my alley. I would go to stores like Barney's, and I would sell them on whatever product we were distributing. At first, it started out small. They would order ten or fifteen copies of this record, ten or so copies of that record. Whatever number of copies that I sold, I would get a percentage. That was great built-in incentive for me to perfect my salesmanship skills. On many occasions, I would be the one who introduced a new record to a radio station and convinced them to play it. As a result of them playing it, that automatically boosted the sales. By the time I got back to the office, Ernie already had orders coming in on the record. Once I began to connect the dots on how the record business worked, there was no turning back.

It's amazing how you can struggle in life for a while, but if you hang in there and don't give up, all of a sudden things start to fall in place. One day somebody asked me, "Carl, didn't you operate that DSJ thing in the service?" I said I had. He informed me that DSJ had an office downtown, and recommended that I go down there. So I followed up on his recommendation, went to DSJ's headquarters, and sure enough, they had a list of people who had bought the exact machine that I became an expert on while in the Air

The Man Behind the Music

Force. As I perused through the list, my eyes almost jumped out of my head when I saw Mr. Al Benson's name. He was the city's top black disc jockey on WGES, and one of the most influential African-American deejays in the country. I immediately went over to his office at 26th and Michigan, and met with him. Fortunately, I made it there just in time because he told me that he was about to send his secretary to school to learn how to operate it. I told him that I was an expert on that very machine. "That's what I did in the Air Force," I enthusiastically emphasized. So having heard that, he hired me right there on the spot. This turned out to be the break that really launched my music career, and the skills I acquired in the Air Force operating the DSJ Composomatic machine prepared me to take advantage of this opportunity.

Al's real name was Arthur B. Leaner, and he originally came from Jackson, Mississippi. He started out as a gospel deejay at WGES in 1943. A couple of years later, he was playing R&B there. Mr. Benson put me to work right away. My job was to create two weekly lists entitled the Top Twenty Songs of the Week and the Top Thirty Up and Coming Records. In each list, we chose one "Pick of the Week" and the "Tune of the Week." We would print three to four hundred copies of this list and distribute them to record stores all over Chicago. That printer that Benson had was one of those old ones that went around and around. Antiquated or not, it kept us in business rolling out hundreds of copies. Each store got at least fifty copies of our weekly list. Sometimes we had to print more, but generally, it was about three hundred, because there were only about five or six stores that really mattered. A few on the Southside, a couple downtown, and of course Barney's on the Westside were my main client stores.

Those lists were like the bible for all the record stores. Whatever the list said, that's what the store owners stocked. If a record label's records and artists weren't on Benson's list, then the record stores and street dealers didn't purchase those records. Al picked the records for his Top Twenty list based on the sales that the stores reported and the requests he received on his daily drive-time radio program, which aired Monday through Saturday on WGES 1390 AM. At the time, WGES was located on the Westside on Washington Boulevard.

Benson was a marketing genius and probably one of the first deejays who would buy time on a radio station such as WGES and then sell it directly to his advertisers, which included many of the local businesses like Parker House Sausage. This practice was known in the radio industry as brokered time. Benson purchased eight hours of programming every day on WGES, but he only broadcast from three to six p.m. He gave the rest of the airtime to three or four black deejays that he liked, including Sam Evans, Sid McCoy, and Lucky Cordell, who in turn would also play the songs from Al's lists. Having that air time gave them the exposure to become popular air personalities in their own right, while playing Al's picks. Everyone benefited: the radio stations, the record labels, the artists, the deejays, and the stores. And everybody got a slice of the pie.

During this time, record companies and distributors were popping up everywhere. South Michigan Avenue was known as Record Row because all the R&B labels and distributors were conveniently concentrated on one strip. If you started at 22nd and Michigan and worked your way ten blocks north to Roosevelt Road, then crossed the street and came back down Michigan to 22nd Street, you could visit nearly every record company in town. Some of these record companies were small companies. Others, were larger companies like RCA Victor and Mercury. It was the same way with the distributors; some were bigger and had more influence than others. But no matter what the size, if a record company's records didn't get enough airtime, they would not sell.

So everything boiled down to airplay. In the radio studio, Al had two boxes that were each filled with 45's: one with the current Top Twenty Songs of the Week and the other with the Thirty Up and Coming Records. He would bring these two boxes in and give them to the engineer, who would take one box and start spinning its contents on the air. Al was famous for his opening line when he went on the air: "Good Afternoon, ladies and gentlemen. This is your old Swingmaster Al Benson bringing you sixty minutes of red hot, beat me down, swing tunes of the day, and that's for sure." When he played all the songs in one box, he'd proceed to the next box and play all the songs that were in it. Mr. Benson would be reading the newspaper with the monitors turned down, and the engineer would tell him what record was going to air next. After the record was over, Benson would close his paper and announce the name of the next artist and continue reading the papers.

Mr. Benson meticulously controlled whose records were played. Depending on their size, Mr. Benson allowed the record companies and distributors to place a certain number of records in his box. The larger the company, the more records you could have in the box. If you were a smaller distributor like Lenny Garmisa, you might have three records. If you were a larger company like All State Distributors, you might have six records. If you were an individual, you'd better have a very hot record and a prayer, and maybe you'd get one record in the box. Anyone who got the opportunity to place a record in the box knew that they had better place their best stuff, or Al would pull that record if no one called about it.

    The distributors would come to me and ask if Al would be willing to exchange some of their records that weren't getting any response. Most of the time, Al would relent and let them exchange the ones that weren't doing too well for ones they felt would do better. However, he never liked them asking to make exchanges on a weekly basis. He felt like they were being too hasty and not giving the records a chance. Al really took pride in the fact that he personally kept up with the progress of their product. He had a system, and it worked. But ironically, he didn't know what the hell he was playing, because most of the time he didn't actually listen to songs that were playing on the air. To him, it was a hit if the phones started ringing and orders were coming in, regardless of what it sounded like.

    There was one other caveat that determined whether you would have a shot at having a record in the box – there was a price to pay. Al had a simple little plan for success: if you paid, your record played. And if you didn't pay, there would be no play. He would pull a record out of rotation immediately. He never told me how much money they paid, but it was enough to make it worthwhile. I would venture to say that it might have been in the neighborhood of a hundred bucks per record, which back in those days was a lot of money. So if you had six records in his box, that meant you might be paying six hundred bucks. You multiply that times ten, whether you're talking about distributors or manufacturers, and he was picking up maybe six thousand dollars a month.

    On top of all that extra income, Al regularly promoted stage shows at the Regal Theater at 47th and South Parkway. The deal was, if he was playing one of your records, then he required that the record company give him that artist free for a show at the Regal. And the best thing in Al's favor was that the label was responsible for paying the artist, not him. Most of the box office receipts, he kept. So once again, Al made a ton of money on the air and on the stage. Mr. Benson was a genius in everything he did, especially when it came to making money off of music.

The Regal Theater was one of the most stylish theaters in Chicago. The theater, both inside and out, was just as majestic as its great name. When you walked in, you couldn't help but notice the Moorish influenced grand lobby, draped in elegant façade. Inside was the famous starlight ceiling that was reminiscent of a beautiful Arabian night. The red velvet curtains that graced the stage were anchored on either side by beautiful golden beams. And the audience nestled on plush red velvet chairs. When black people came to the Regal Theater, they all felt like dignitaries.

The stage shows back in those days were not like concert settings that you find today. They were respectful events – no guns, no gangs, and no dope smoking. They usually had early and late shows. Families came to the early evening shows. Mothers brought their sons, fathers brought their daughters, and sweethearts cuddled together for a wholesome night of dazzling entertainment. Before the show started, they always played a cartoon, and then a movie. After the movie was finished, the people would automatically start cheering in anticipation of the concert about to start. Once those huge red velvet curtains fell over the movie screen and you could hear the band tuning up, the palpable excitement automatically started to build.

As employees of Benson's, Skeets Van Horn and I got to be a part of his shows there at the Regal. We were just gofers, doing whatever Al wanted us to do. As a matter of fact, we wanted to be down there more than he needed us, but Al didn't mind. Al would make the dressing room assignments for all the acts coming in. So as the groups started arriving, Skeets and I would be backstage, directing them towards their respective dressing rooms. The A-room was the nicest and had more amenities. That was for the headliners. The B-room was for everyone else.

Being backstage for one of Al's stage shows was the place to be. It was so exciting. I began to meet all those big stars personally: Louis Armstrong, Lena Horne, Count Basie, Jackie Wilson, and many more. However, the one that stuck out in my mind more than any of them was Jackie Wilson. I was a big fan of Jackie's before I ever recorded him. He had this habit of licking his lips all the time. I guess it was just one of those strange idiosyncrasies. Whenever Jackie Wilson was around, there would always be a whole lotta shakin' going on. There would always be a line of girls outside his

The Man Behind the Music

dressing room waiting to get in to see him. When you walked by his dressing room, you'd hear the passionate moans and groans of Jackie and one of those girls having sex. Next thing you know, one of these ladies would be coming out of his room, fixing herself up, and then Jackie would stick his head out of the room and beckon for the next girl to come in. I would just shake my head and say, "Man, whata guy." Jackie Wilson was something else.

Mr. Benson presented all the hottest talent on his shows. He had greats like James Brown, Sam Cooke, the Treniers, Dinah Washington, Ruth Brown, and even comedians like Moms Mabley. All of them got their start right there at the Regal. However, with all their musical genius and gifted artistry, many of these artists could not read or write a note of music. They had hit records, but they had no written arrangements. This could be a problem when you had a live orchestra behind you. So the night before the performance, they would give their records to the band leader and drummer Red Saunders, and he would go home that night and score out the music for his orchestra.

Al would be the emcee for all the shows. And being the great radio personality that he was, he was a master emcee. With Al on stage introducing each act, he would have the audience sitting on the edge of their seats. As the audience's excitement reached a crescendo, the place would be absolutely electrified. Depending on who the artist was, you would need some crowd control, because women would try to rush the stage. To keep everything under control backstage, Al hired a Chicago cop we nicknamed "Lock 'Em Up Jones." If you didn't belong back stage, Jones would run you from back there in a hot second. People would try to sneak in through the alley entrance, because that's where the backstage door was located. If you didn't belong back there, Jones would throw your butt out in a heartbeat, or even have you locked up.

During this period of my career, Al wasn't paying me a lot of money, but working for him was a priceless opportunity to make a lot of contacts and learn the business. I met all the key people from big labels like RCA Victor, Mercury, Capitol, Roulette, and Savoy, as well as local distributors Lenny Garmisa, Milt Salstone, and Ewart Abner, one of the main men at Chicago's Vee-Jay Records. Key record executives, A&R men, and promoters would come to Chicago from all over the country to meet with Al Benson. Whenever this one executive would come to town to see Al, he would have me take him around to the different stores. This guy would always show his appreciation by rolling up a crisp one-hundred dollar bill and sticking it in my coat pocket. Escorting this guy around town was a privilege, but getting a c-note for a tip, too, that was the icing on the cake.

All the good times and nightlife were fine and dandy in their place, but you couldn't forget the fact that this was the music business. I was more interested in making the real money, so I quickly learned the ends and the outs of the inner workings of the music business machine. While I was working for Al Benson, I had a great vantage point. I was compiling those weekly Top Twenty surveys for Al by combining the requests from the radio station and the sales from the stores. I would call all the record shops and get their Top Ten lists. No matter how many stores there were, I'd call them all.

Once I had their stats, I'd compare those to the requests that came in during Benson's WGES shows. From those numbers, I could determine the ranking of one through twenty. Wow, I was in the mix. I was playing a key role in a record's ranking. This was a powerful position to be in. Al Benson was the vehicle, but I had become the driver. The up-and-coming artists and records, I used to work those any way I wanted to do them. And the people were willing to show their appreciation for however I wanted to place their product.

Sometimes I'd get a call directly from someone who had an out of town label, maybe in New York or Philadelphia. These labels would usually negotiate a deal by asking that I place their product in the up-and-coming list, and I'd be more than happy to accommodate them. Sometimes the guy would send me a money order, or maybe a box of stock records that I could turn around and sell to stores like Barney's. I liked the fact that in the music business, there were multiple ways of making money.

After finding my niche in dealing with the Top Thirty Up and Coming Records, I had to develop my skills in predicting which of these could make it to the regular Top Twenty list. Therefore, after I finished work, I would take a stack of these Up and Coming records home with me, listen to them, and make my predictions. At first, my averages weren't too good. My picks were twenty percent right and eighty percent wrong. However, I stuck with it and after a year or so, I flipped those averages and was now picking eighty percent right. In the course of a year, I had sharpened my skills to such a degree that I could pick a hit eight out of ten times.

The Man Behind the Music

Before I got there, Mr. Benson had already gotten his feet wet with operating his own record labels. From 1952 through 1956, he owned Parrot and Blue Lake labels, but he got weary with that end of the record business and got out altogether. However, that didn't stop all these wannabe stars from coming to Al's office with songs they wanted him to hear in hopes he could help make them a star. "Al, listen to this. I know you're gonna love it," they'd all promise. Al wasn't the kind of guy who relished dashing someone's dreams. So most of the time, he'd grin and bear it. But a lot of these people weren't worth listening to. They had little lead sheets, or lyric sheets, and they'd sing A cappella and try humming the melody. But no matter how hard they tried to get Al to become interested in them, he didn't have time for that any more. Besides, he was too busy making a killing playing records on the radio for all the different manufacturers and promoting shows at the Regal.

This presented a unique opportunity for me. I had already proven to be good at picking hit records, so I knew I could also pick a hit artist. What Al didn't want to do, became my inroad to success. I started listening to some of these young acts, and I heard a few promising ones that I thought were very good. I stumbled right into something that would eventually catapult me to the top of the music business. It was at that defining moment in my music business career that I became involved in producing. Benson told me to go ahead if I wanted to do something with those newcomers. So with his blessing, I stepped into a whole new role that would change the course of my life forever.

Even though I had been bitten by the producing bug, I still wasn't in the money yet. Therefore, I had to get a part-time job to keep a couple extra bucks in my pocket. In 1958, I met this cool white boy named William "Bunky" Sheppard, who worked at a company on Wabash Avenue called Favor Ruhl. They made frames for pictures and mattes. He got me a job as his helper there. Bunky was born in New Orleans and swore up and down that he was black. Though he was obviously white, I never challenged him on it. I just went along with him. Bunky told me that his mother was a hooker, and that they used to live in a house-of-ill-repute in the red-light section of town. The way I figured it, maybe many of his mother's johns were black, so Bunky grew up thinking that he, too, was black. But whatever the case, he talked and acted just like he was a brother.

Carl H. Davis, Sr.

I'm not sure how he found out that I had ties to Al Benson, but one day he told me that he was doing some things in the music business. Man, no matter where I turned, I kept bumping into people who were associated with the music business. As it turned out, Bunky managed a really good Chicago vocal group called the Sheppards. Evidently, they were named after him. They had already cut a single titled "Island of Love." I listened to it and I liked it. I really liked it. Once he saw that I thought his group was pretty good, he asked me if I would ask Al Benson to play it. I quickly told him "I don't know. I ain't in that part of the thing." I couldn't make him no promises.

Apparently, that wasn't the answer that he wanted to hear, because one day he showed up at the radio station unannounced with a bottle of gin in his hand, wanting to see Al. Old Bunky must have gotten his people and places mixed up. We weren't at the factory. He was in my element now, and I told him, "Don't you dare go in there and insult Al Benson like that. You can't impress him with no liquor. If it's liquor he wants, he don't have to get it from you. He'll get it himself!" Bunky was a little embarrassed and felt like he might have just stepped in some dog poop. But he was alright with me, so I took the record and got Al to put it on the air, and it turned out to do moderately well. This was a huge favor to Bunky.

"Island Of Love" was released on a Chicago label named Apex Records, right off of 47th Street and Drexel. Bunky was real tight with its owner, Dempsey Nelson, who also owned a cleaning service bearing the same name. I don't know whether Dempsey gave Bunky some ownership in the company, but it's a possibility that he did, because Bunky would go out and beat the pavement promoting the company's new releases. That's how he got acquainted with most of the disc jockeys around the country.

Bunky and I hit it off very well and we became inseparable. We both shared the same ideology on the music business. After a while, I really started believing that Bunky might indeed have some soul-brother running through his blood because he had rhythm and swagger just like a black man. We collaborated on various acts and songs, all while we held on to our day jobs. He lived not that far from me. Everybody liked Bunky. He was the kind of person that you wouldn't mind doing anything for. He lived at 78th and Calumet, and I was living at 77th and Rhodes. We used to go by each other's house. Our families would have dinner together. We'd watch the ball games

The Man Behind the Music

and also shoot pool at the local tavern. Wherever you saw Bunky, you saw me, and vice-versa. Bunky was the rare thing that few of us experience, but everyone wishes they had – a true friend.

By this time, I had gotten to know all the distributors up and down South Michigan Avenue. And all those record companies would send me their records to make sure I'd put their songs on the list. That always meant that I would get a few dollars here, and a few dollars there.

In 1959, Morry Price, President of Arnold Distributing, offered me a position as the promotions representative for the rhythm and blues stations. This was a job opportunity that I had been looking for for a long time, and it paid well. My only concern was whether Al would let me go. I knew this could be a very sensitive issue with Al. He wasn't exactly the guy you wanted to piss off in this business. So I had to come to him in a diplomatic way. I told him, "As much as I appreciated being here at the station with you, working over at Arnold Distributing gives me a chance to make a better salary. But I still need the benefits of our good relationship in order for me to be successful in my new job. So I wanted to get your permission to take this job." Al's blessing was key to me making this move, because I still had to come to him with Arnold's records to get them played. Al, being the shrewd businessman that he was, said, "The only way I'll give you permission is if you continue to put out my Top Twenty sheet for me." No problem. I would take that concession any day because I could put my own stuff on the list, too. So I readily agreed, and went over to Arnold, while I still put out Al's Top Twenty list.

Although it was a new company, Arnold distributed quite a few out-of-town labels, including Jubilee, Shad, Golden Crest, Ric, Ron, and Amy. In the past, they hadn't had much success getting their records played at all, but because of my relationship with Al Benson, their records were getting air time. Arnold also distributed Morris Levy's Roulette label out of New York. So whenever their artists came to town to visit with local deejays Sid McCoy and Marty Faye, I got to escort artists like Count Basie and Maynard Ferguson around.

One of the greatest jazz producers of that time was Teddy Reig. Teddy, who was known for his colorful and lively character, came to Chicago to produce some records for Roulette by Basie and his orchestra. Count Basie and I had some great times together. I used to take him out to

Carl H. Davis, Sr.

Hawthorn Park right off Cicero Avenue because he loved playing the ponies. He never won that much money, but I guess it was the thrill of betting on his favorite horse that excited him. One night I decided to go down to Universal Recording Studios while Teddy and Basie were recording. I went by just to see how things were going. This particular session was an all-nighter. The renowned jazz baritone soloist Joe Williams and Basie's orchestra cut "Five O'Clock In The Morning." Ironically, it was actually five o'clock in the morning when they got around to doing Joe's vocals.

Working at Arnold Distributing marked the first time that I promoted a record head-to-head against my good friend Granville (Granny)White, local promotion manager for Columbia Records. A swinging dance called the Madison was sweeping the country in 1960. I was promoting "The Madison" by Al Brown's Tunetoppers on the New York-based Amy label, and Granny was pushing jazz pianist Ray Bryant's "The Madison Time" on Columbia. I outsold him locally, although Bryant ended up with the bigger national record. I went to the radio stations around Chicago and got mine on their playlists first, and they started playing it. So that kind of proved that I had the right record, or the right ear. Granville and I were like brothers. I used to tell him, "My 'Madison' is much better than yours!" He'd retort saying, "We'll see!" But we had good spirits about it and we never fell out because we were too tight, and it was just business.

From Arnold Distributing, I briefly moved over to Summit Distributing on West Diversey Parkway on Chicago's Northside. But shortly after that, another door of opportunity opened up for me at Columbia. In 1960, I ended up replacing Granville as Columbia's local promotion manager. It was a strange twist of fate. Granny was promoted to being Columbia's regional promotions man, but right after he got settled into that position, something happened with Columbia's national guy. As a result, they brought Granny to New York and made him the national promotion man. However, he never really accepted the job on a permanent basis. He took it temporarily until they could find someone else. At the time, Granny didn't want to be stuck in an office and involved in all the New York corporate politics. He loved being out and about, promoting the artists and meeting the jocks.

I still remember the times when I used to go on the road with Granville to places like Charlotte, North Carolina and all those other places in the South where black folks weren't allowed to stay overnight at a hotel.

The Man Behind the Music

In most of these places, you had to hit the highway and go out far beyond city limits in order to find a hotel where blacks could spend the night. But it didn't matter where we went; Granny had a thick telephone book packed with the names of disc jockeys and everybody else you might want to meet.

I really enjoyed all the experiences that I had with Granville. He taught me everything there was to know about promotions, and I'll never forget the times we spent together. Over the years as I moved up in the record business, I used to help him out a lot, too. No favor was too much for him to ask. Granny had a very illustrious career as a promotions executive, with numerous awards for his outstanding service and contributions to the music industry. Granville and I remained best of friends he until passed away in 1997.

Although becoming Columbia's local promotions man was a great opportunity as well as being a coveted rung in the ladder of my success, it was also the nemesis to my marriage, which began to suffer greatly as I chased my career aspirations. In 1954 when June and I were married, I wasn't in the music business. I was fresh out of the military trying to find my place in the world, and I stumbled into the music business. But six years later, I was waist deep in my budding career and I was at a point where I compromised the most important thing in my life at the time, my marriage. I still feel guilty about it to this day. My sweet little wife and I had a wonderful relationship, full of joy and passion. Over the years, as I got more involved in the business, she put up with a lot (long hours and late nights), but she never really complained.

However, once I accepted the job at Columbia, I concocted a little scheme to get out of my marriage. I told June that I had this great opportunity to go to work for Columbia Records, and that it was a records promotions job where I'd be traveling all over the country. I went on to say it would look much better if I weren't married. I told her that if we could get a divorce and I accepted the position, then I could come back and remarry her – but this wasn't true and I knew it. Unfortunately, as sweet as June was, she was equally gullible, and she believed my deceptive ruse.

Eventually she found out that I lied to her and, understandably, she became very upset with me. June never did anything to deserve such treatment. All of this was a result of my own self-centered ambition and a misguided desire for success. Even though June and I have moved far beyond this issue, to this day, there is still a twinge of lingering guilt that occasionally haunts me. As a way to compensate for my misdeed, I have always tried to be as supportive as I could. I made sure she had money to take care of herself and the kids. I bought her a three-flat building where she lived rent-free. And I used my connections with the late John Stroger, who was a friend of mine and later became the president of the Cook County Board, to get her a career job with the Cook County Sheriff's Department. After thirty years of dedicated service, she retired with a very comfortable pension. June now lives in a senior citizens building in downtown Chicago. To this day, if we have any kind of family gathering or special event, she comes out and joins us. She's like a sister to me, and I still love her and she still loves me.

  Later on that year, Skeets Van Orn introduced me to another young lady named Mabel Cummings. We met at Al Benson's office after Skeets brought her there to visit. We hit it off right away, fell in love, and before 1960 was over, I was married again. Three years later in 1963, we had our first son, Carl H. Davis, Jr.

  Soon after getting remarried, in 1961 Bunky and I launched our own production company called, Pam Productions, which was affectionately named after my first daughter. We also formed the Pam label and released several singles, including records by the Sheppards. Artists in our line-up included a blues singer named Lucky Carmichael and a couple of lesser known acts that Bunky produced, but I have no specific recollection of them. However, we did have a national hit "Better Tell Him No," by a local female group named the Starlets. Their lead singer was Maxine Edwards, and the rest of the group consisted of Dynetta Boone, Jane Hall, Mickey McKinney, and Jeannette Miles. "Better Tell Him No" was on Billboard's pop charts for sixteen weeks in the spring of '61, and was an even bigger R&B hit.

  The Starlets were managed by Bernice Williams, a young lady who lived in this big old frame house around 59th and Lafayette. Besides being a manager, she was also a prolific writer with a lot of range and a large catalog of songs. With all the success that "Better Tell Him No" brought us, the Starlets were able to hit the road to perform. They hit many of the Chitlin' Circuit stops, making their way all the way to Philadelphia. While there, a car dealer named Harold Robinson (who had a small label there called Newtown) coaxed the Starlets into the studio. Somehow, while all that was transpiring, one of his artists, Patti LaBelle, persuaded the Starlets to do the background vocals on "I Sold My Heart To The Junkman," while Patti did the lead. This was an outrage. He used our girls to do the background vocals on his record without our permission.

To make matters even worse, "Junkman" came out on Newtown as Patti LaBelle and the Blue-Belles when it was really the Starlets that sang background. The song became a massive pop and R&B hit during the spring of 1962. Bunky and I were livid, and we sued Harold Robinson and Newtown Records, and won. After it was all said and done, we only got a few dollars out of it, but that was alright. It was the principle of the matter. They knew they weren't supposed to record a group that was under contract to someone else. But this is a dog-eat-dog business, where label owners with cutthroat mentalities unfortunately were a dime a dozen.

The Starlets had one other Pam single, "Money Hungry," that Bernice wrote right before we folded the label, although Pam Productions remained quite active for some time after that. By mid-1962, I was working for Columbia's OKeh subsidiary, and we released one more Starlets single there, but it wasn't long after that the Starlets' light fizzled out and died.

Bunky and I formed a couple of other short-lived labels during this same period. Wes Records was named for the initials of William E. Sheppard, while Nat Records was named after our bookkeeper, whose first name was Nathaniel. Wes only lasted for a handful of releases that were Bunky's doing, the best-known being the Sheppards' beautiful "Glitter In Your Eyes."

In my career in the record business, whenever things didn't seem to be happening the way I thought they should be – whenever the cards weren't falling right or the dominoes weren't lining up – it wouldn't be long before another door of opportunity would eventually open. Sometimes it would be a phone call or a knock at the door. In this business, you have to be fast on your feet, and seize opportunities whenever they present themselves. I learned to master how to recognize a golden opportunity. In this case, the gateway to success came in the form of a magical little melody that would translate into Pam Productions' first real smash hit.

Chapter 3

The 1960s were a very interesting time in our nation's history. Though the foul winds of racial segregation blew vehemently across the arid social terrain, yet the sweet aroma of change and equality added a pleasant fragrance to the pungent resistance to equality. But no matter what the state of affairs of race relations, there was something that always seemed to unite this otherwise polarized society – that was music emanating out from the black community. Just as Chicago was a unique and majestic city, so the Chicago sound was unique and majestic. The Chicago sound captured the grit of the black struggle but was tempered with the melodic and poetical ideals of love, happiness and hope for a brighter tomorrow.

During this time, there were many budding acts popping up all over the place. Young kids with stardom gleaming in their eyes practiced and rehearsed to prepare for that one defining moment that would lead them from singing in their basements and living rooms at home, to the spotlights and glamour of venues like the Regal and Apollo theaters. Such was the case of a talented young group that came from the Englewood community on Chicago's Southside. They were called the Dukays. As I stated earlier, there were many groups that would come to Al Benson's office to show their talent in hopes of getting Al's interest to get them a record deal. Since Al really wasn't interested, I did all the listening. The Dukays were one of the young talented R&B vocal groups that came up to Al's office. They did a few tunes and I liked what I heard. They were the first act that I really became interested in on a personal level. They had a charming and charismatic lead singer named Eugene Dixon. The rest of the Dukays' members were his cousin Shirley Jones, who sang first tenor, second tenor James Lowe, baritone Earl Edwards (the brother of Maxine from the Starlets), and bass singer Ben Broyles.

Bernice Williams was their manager and she was writing most of their songs. They even rehearsed at her home on the Southside. By this time, Bernice was known for being a prolific songwriter, and she was certainly one of the heavyweights in town, providing material for several groups. One day Bunky and I met with the Dukays. We listened to some of their material and discussed some business issues. After that meeting, Bunky and I agreed that this group had great potential and that there was something special about them. However, one of the things that was still necessary was to fine tune their sound, which required some musical orchestration. But we didn't have any lead sheets for their material. This is when I went to my brother Clifford and I asked him to do the lead sheets for the group.

Years ago, when I was growing up and living over on 69th and Langley, my older brother Clifford had already enlisted in the Navy. Clifford was naturally musically inclined and played in the Navy band. I imagine his musical genes came from my mother's side of the family. Clifford was multi-talented and played several instruments, like the saxophone, the vibes and the piano. When he came home after being discharged, he started playing up on 63rd Street at the Pershing Ballroom. Clifford also played at the Cotton Club, which at that time, was located on 62nd and Cottage Grove. Clifford was a heck of a saxophone player, and always had a gig going on somewhere.

Even though I was underage, I used to sneak into the Cotton Club and watch him while he played. Then at the Pershing Ballroom, they used to have the battle of the bands. Some of the city's finest jazz bands would go heads up at these informal competitions. Clifford would be playing against Sonny Stitt and Gene Ammons. Each saxophonist would belt out great solos consisting of phenomenal riffs and complex scales. It was a great competition. One band would win one week, another band would win the following week, but Clifford would usually come out on top. By the late '50s, Clifford was in such high demand on the local studio scene that he was consistently doing R&B sessions as a tenor saxophonist for the Chess and Vee-Jay records.

That's Cliff soloing on Rosco Gordon's 1960 Vee-Jay smash "Just A Little Bit," and he had four '59 instrumental singles of his own on the Federal label with his band, the Turbo-Jets. Cliff was cutting tracks on some of everybody's records. It seemed like every time you heard a saxophone solo on a Chicago-cut R&B record, it was Clifford. And make no mistake about it; every time you heard a tenor sax solo on one of my productions, it was my brother Clifford.

So Clifford wrote out the lead sheets and the chord changes for me, and we went in the studio and recorded the Dukays. Bernice wrote their debut single for release on our Nat label, "The Girl's A Devil," which became a pop hit during the spring and summer of 1961, with Bernice's ballad "The Big Lie" on the flip side.

We were scheduled to do another Dukays session at Universal Recording Corporation at 46 E. Walton, the city's premier recording studio. I believe our engineer was Bob Kidder, with whom we had four tunes scheduled for recording. Bunky and I were in the office and the Dukays were out there singing this line that I thought was very catchy. They kept singing this "doo, doo, doo" repetition.

I asked, "Hey what is that?"

They replied nonchalantly, "Oh, this is a little something for the next session."

I knew a hit melody when I heard it. I had become proficient at picking songs that were commercial successes. I wasn't letting this opportunity slip through my hands. This "little something," as they referred to it, was not an option.

I replied emphatically, "Oh, no, no, no. That ain't no little something. Whatever that is, it's a smash. And you are doing that on today's session, or there won't be no session!"

After I said that, Eugene, Shirley, James and Edward all shrugged their shoulders and replied, "We ain't even got no lyrics or nothing to this. All we have right now is the line 'doo, doo, doo.' It's not even a song yet."

The Man Behind the Music

I realized at that point that they didn't know what they had. This melody was a diamond in the rough, so it was my job to put them under the gun and pull a hit out of them.

I said, "Well, go home and get with Bernice!"

They went to Bernice's house, where they rehearsed, and they started writing the lyrics. Later on that night, they called me at home, and they asked me a question that I thought was rather strange.

They asked, "If a guy is a king and he owns a lot of land, what is it?"

I replied, " I guess it would be a kingdom."

Then they asked, "What if he's a duke?"

I said, "Well, it would have to be a dukedom!"

"That's good, we'll call you back later," they replied, then abruptly hung up the phone.

I could hear the excitement in their voices. Something clicked when I said dukedom. I wasn't sure what it was, but they finished writing the song and got it ready to record. I gave it to Clifford, and he did the lead sheets. We went into Universal, and we cut two smokers on the group, "Nite Owl" and "Kissin' In The Kitchen." The latter featured one of Clifford's signature alto sax solos. We also slowed the pace down a bit and recorded a mellow ballad called "Festival Of Love." Last but not least, that song that had no name, no lyrics, no nothing, that they put together at my behest, was called "Duke Of Earl." The "Earl" part of the song title came from Earl Edwards' name, who also shared in the writers' credit with Gene and Bernice. All four songs were recorded during the same recording session and they all came out great.

The Nat label was being nationally distributed by Bill Lasley's Lesgal Productions in New York. We sent him all four songs. Lasley listened to all four, and he said, "Naw, I just want 'Nite Owl'." And he also kept "Festival of Love" as the flipside. He sent back "Duke Of Earl" and "Kissin' In The Kitchen." We made the decision to release "Nite Owl" and "Festival Of Love" on the Nat label by the Dukays. "Nite Owl" ended up being a national pop hit during the early weeks of 1962. I liked "Nite Owl," but I really wanted to get "Duke Of Earl" released, too. However, it was imperative that I come up with the right marketing strategy in order to maximize its appeal and sales potential. I felt a single artist approach for this song would be much better, where the song's theme could be centered around the artist.

I called a meeting with the whole group. I asked them if we could release the remaining two songs under the name of Eugene Dixon, the lead singer. As a compromise, I promised the group that they all would share the entire benefits of all four sides. It wasn't that hard to convince Gene to go solo because he always imagined himself as a solo artist anyway. It was a harder sell for the others because we had talked so much about unity and staying together no matter what – now this contradicted all that. Besides, doing it this way gave us two acts for two separate hits, by the same group. As a marketing angle, this was the better route to go.

Once the Dukays agreed, the next obstacle we faced was coming up with a good stage name for Eugene. There wasn't a lot of stage appeal to Eugene Dixon, even though it was his real name. I said, "I don't like that at all." His first name, we needed to work on, but his last name had to go completely.

One of my favorite actors at the time was Jeff Chandler. He played Cochise in the classic western film "Broken Arrow." I had an epiphany. "That's it," I exclaimed. I said, "Why don't we do this? We'll drop the first part of your name and just call you Gene. Then we'll throw on Chandler as your last name." We all loved it, and everybody agreed. At that very defining moment in music history, a new star was born, Mr. Gene Chandler. We released "Duke of Earl," performed by Gene Chandler, and the rest is music history. Soon, Gene Chandler was a household name. And even though it started out as a pseudonym, I believe he had his name legally changed to Gene Chandler.

I didn't know anybody up at Vee-Jay Records yet, but Bunky did. Vee-Jay was Chicago's second biggest R&B label after Chess. Bunky knew their A&R man Calvin Carter, who was co-owner Vivian Carter's brother. Vivian was the "Vee" and Jimmy Bracken was the "Jay" in Vee-Jay. So he took it up there, and Calvin fell in love with "Duke Of Earl." Ewart Abner, who was running the company, was in England right then. Calvin called Abner in England and said, "Man, Carl and Bunky have come up with a smash! I want to pick it up." Abner said, "Go ahead, if you think it's a smash. Pick it up!" We asked him for $30,000, which isn't a lot by today's standards, but back then, it was a lot of money. So by the end of October of 1961, Vee-Jay picked up "Duke of Earl." On February 17, 1962, "Duke of Earl" was officially the number one pop record in the entire country. It sat at the top of the R&B charts for five weeks.

Since I was still employed at Columbia when we cut "Duke of Earl," I didn't put my name down as the producer. Even though I was the impetus behind the project, I told Bunky to put his name on it just in case it hits, then it would be easier for him to get a job. I was doing alright because I already had a job. By this time, he wasn't working at Favor Ruhl anymore, and he wasn't with Apex Records, which had closed its doors.

After Bunky and I produced "Duke Of Earl," it brought us some serious credibility. We were the hottest new producing stars on the block. As a result of all the recognition, Vee-Jay Records gave Bunky a job as a promotions man. It wasn't long after that all the hoopla over "Duke of Earl" reached the Big Apple, where Bill Lasley of Lesgal Productions was. When Bill found out that "Duke Of Earl" was by Eugene Dixon and the Dukays, he tried to weasel his way into our pockets and tried to threaten us with the notion that he was supposed to have all four of those masters. We weren't buying any of that crap at all. I quickly reminded him in some very specific terms that this was not the case. We offered "Duke of Earl" to him, and he flat-out turned all the tunes down and only kept "Nite Owl" and "Festival of Love." I can imagine that he must have been sick over this, but I didn't have time to be hearing that foolishness – business is business.

The massive success of "Duke of Earl" meant my chart tabulating days with Al Benson were over, too. I told him that I wouldn't be able to do the sheet for him any longer. But Al being Al always had a way of cutting a deal that benefited him, so he suggested that I at least come in and set up the machine so the girls could print out the list. This wasn't a real problem for me because by that time, I had gotten pretty close to the girls up there at his office, and I showed them how to operate the machine so they were able to do it themselves. In the summer of '62, Al Benson's historic reign on WGES ended anyway. Gordon McLendon bought the station, scrapped all of the brokered shows that featured some of Chicago's top deejays, including Al's, and instituted a Top 40 format. That was a bad move and considerably less successful with WGES's fan base.

After the production of "Duke of Earl," I assumed personal management of Gene Chandler. For one event, we brought Gene out to San Francisco to do a benefit show. We flew out there on American Airlines.

However, the promoters arranged it so that when the plane landed, the pilot would taxi over to a tarmac off the runway. They had us get off the American Airlines plane and we boarded another private plane. "Where the hell are we going now?" I thought. We got on the private plan, but it didn't take off. Instead it pulled around to a designated gate, and to our surprise, there were at least two thousand screaming fans waiting out there with these signs that read "Duke of Earl" and "Duchess of Earl." I had never seen anything like that. To add to all of the media glitz and glamour, Gene came off the plane in his tux, top hat, and cape, which he wore to play the role of the Duke of Earl.

    Wearing the Duke's costume was not my idea. Gene came up with all of that. There was no doubt about it, Gene was a genius when it came to ideas concerning his career and the music business. Maybe that's why we didn't get along too well back in those days, because he was so cocky. He was so sure of himself, and I was so sure of myself, too. Looking back on it, his assertiveness was a good thing because he made some very wise financial and career decisions. Lord have mercy, we seemed to argue about everything. The only thing we really didn't argue a lot about was things concerning our music relationship.

    Back then, I asked myself whether he was worth all of the problems he caused. But I must admit, Gene often had some very good ideas, although my hot head got in the way sometimes, and I didn't always listen to him. I couldn't really knock him when we didn't see eye-to-eye because he knew what he wanted to do and how to go about doing it. Today, Gene and I are friends and we have many cherished memories between us. If there were ever any hard feeling between us, it's all water under the bridge now.

    With the $25,000 that I earned from "Duke Of Earl," Mabel and I bought a brand new home at 87th and Calumet. Bunky received the same amount, and the Dukays, including Gene Chandler, got about $50,000 and divided it amongst the members of the group. Bunky went out and splurged, buying us ten suits apiece, with shirts and pants, plus a lot of mohair. We rode high on the hog for a while, until we folded the Nat label because we never got paid for "Nite Owl" – at least I never did.

    I gave Mabel the check for $25,000. She took $20,000 of it and gave me back five. It was Mabel who supervised the building of our house. When they were pouring the concrete for the foundation, she would go to the donut

The Man Behind the Music

shop and get ten or fifteen cups of coffee and a box of doughnuts, and she would pass it all out to the guys who were working on the foundation. At first, I didn't understand why she would go through all that trouble. But to my surprise, I found out that a few cups of coffee and some donuts go a long way with contractors. Needless to say, we never had a leak in our foundation, but the other houses on our block had leaks.

As a result of the mammoth success of "Duke of Earl," in 1962, I got hired as a producer by Columbia Records' A&R department. With that move, I saw an open door to leave Gene in the hands of Bunky and Calvin Carter, which I did. They went in the studio and did "Walk on with the Duke." Vee-Jay released it as a recording by the Duke of Earl rather than by Gene Chandler. Apparently their marketing angle was to capitalize off of the "Duke of Earl" success. This was a terrible marketing plan that was a twofold mistake. First of all, the record should have been released in Gene Chandler's name, not in his character's name. To me, calling him Duke of Earl was too condescending, and it typecast him into a persona that was much too narrow for his wide range of talent. After all, we went through all that trouble coming up with the dad-gum name of Gene Chandler, and I didn't want it overshadowed. Secondly, "Walk on with the Duke" was a bad song. It was terribly ill-conceived and did not go over well with Gene's fan base.

One day, the telephone rang and it was Gene. He was very upset, saying words to this effect: "You are my manager. Why do you have me doing all this crap with Calvin and Bunky? They don't know what the hell they're doing. I want you to produce me, not them." I definitely understood where he was coming from. After that last fiasco, I couldn't blame him. So I told him that I would, but I wouldn't be able to put my name on it, because I was still with Columbia.

So that's when I went to Curtis Mayfield, who would write most of Gene's next batch of hits. However, I co-wrote a ballad called "You Left Me" with Bunky and Gene that came out on Vee-Jay in 1962. "You Left Me" came about as a result of me and Bunky going out to California. I was on the plane one day, seated in first class, when I met this very lovely stewardess. She and I started talking and it seemed like we talked all the way to Los Angles. I told her what hotel we were staying at, fully intending to have a romantic tryst. The day that she did call me, we were going out to do some

Carl H. Davis, Sr.

TV show, and I wasn't able to get with her. She was only in town for three or four days before she left and went back east somewhere, and I never saw her again. A little heartbroken that I had blown a blissful encounter with this beautiful woman, thinking of her, I sat down and started writing the song "You Left Me."

In late '62, we got our first follow-up hit record on Gene and it turned out to be a two-sider – where both sides were a hit. The original A-side was "You Threw A Lucky Punch," an answer to Mary Wells' Motown smash "You Beat Me To The Punch." Our version had a similar melody and beat, but the lyrics were from the man's perspective. After the deejays wore that side out, they flipped it over to the B-side and Gene's rendition of Curtis Mayfield's "Rainbow" proved to be an even bigger seller in early '63. It was Gene Chandler who made it the hit that it turned out to be. The whole concept about Rainbow's performance was all his. Gene had another R&B hit that summer with Curtis' "Man's Temptation." This was one of my favorites. On this song, I used Johnny Pate, who played the up-right bass, as the arranger. One night after his band was finished playing a set, he called me off to the side and said, "Carl, I'm an arranger. Give me a shot!" And I gladly told him that I would. When we got ready to do the Gene Chandler date, I went out to his house, I sounded out the melodies as best as I could, and told him what I was hearing with the rhythm section. That was all that I needed to do. This young man was a brilliant arranger, because from my crude renditions, he gave me back a polished arrangement that was out of sight. From that debut arrangement that he did on Gene's record, he ended up becoming one of the top R&B arrangers in Chicago.

Though there were many record company giants in the country at the time, there weren't that many black owned record labels that were considered big time. However, Vee-Jay was the top black-owned record label in Chicago and one of the biggest in the country. They had a very impressive talent roster, including hit makers like Jerry Butler, Dee Clark, Jimmy Reed, the Spaniels, and the Dells, long before Gene joined the roster.

Even though many of the black promotion men in town worked for other companies, everybody wanted to be in on what Vee-Jay had going on. They might be busy doing their own jobs during the day, but they'd find a way to get over there to Vee-Jay at five or six o'clock in the evening. Not only could they keep a pulse on what's going on in the industry, but they

The Man Behind the Music

also went up to Vee-Jay to socialize, have a drink and unwind. Some even stayed until after midnight. The fact is, even though during the day we may have all been fierce competitors, at the same time, there was still a camaraderie and a respect for Vee-Jay. Vee-Jay represented the level of success and prestige that we as black people wanted to achieve. So here in Chicago, Vee-Jay was the top black-owned label that gave us all a sense of pride.

Anybody who was in the business, whether they were local or from out of town, would come hang out at Vee-Jay Records. Vee-Jay had an employee lounge that turned into a nightspot after working hours. Industry personalities would be up there trading stories and shooting the breeze, while others would be playing cards. The people who didn't want to gamble would sit around the makeshift bar, which was really a lunchroom counter, and have a few drinks. Ewart Abner would be right in there sitting in his chair with his legs crossed. I'll never forget the way he used to shake his leg as he intensely concentrated on his poker game. He was really good at playing poker and he loved to gamble. However, poker became an obsession and the vise that eventually ruined his relationship with Vee-Jay Records.

Anyone who was a part of that scene, wherever you went, after you promoted your own product, you would always mention Vee-Jay too. Vee-Jay had the luxury of having everybody promoting Vee-Jay. Vee-Jay set the standard. Knowing what was going on at Vee-Jay kept you in the know. That was just the way it was. We all took some pride in the fact that it was *the* black record company, and to even be indirectly affiliated with them gave us all welcomed credibility. No one ever suggested that we had to do it, but we did it willingly because everybody wants to be connected to a winner, and Vee-Jay was a winner.

When Abner originally signed Gene Chandler, he signed him to a personal services contract. Technically, this meant that Gene was with Abner, not Vee-Jay, even though Gene's records were coming out on the Vee-Jay label. This would turn out to be a prudent move, because in August of 1963, the relationship between Vee-Jay and Abner suddenly soured, due to Abner's bad gambling habits. Vee-Jay heads Jimmy Bracken and Vivian Carter fired Abner because he went to Las Vegas and chalked up thousands of dollars in gambling debts, then wrote a Vee-Jay check to cover his losses. Jimmy and Vivian were livid. To add insult to injury, since Gene was under a personal services contract with Abner, Abner took Gene with him. Although he was fired from Vee-Jay, Abner took this sour lemon situation and made some sweet lemonade of his own. He joined forces with Bunky, who had been doing promotion and A&R for Vee-Jay, and launched Constellation Records, right under Vee-Jay's nose, and even set up Constellation's office right down the street from Vee-Jay's headquarters. As a result, Gene Chandler, who used to be one of Vee-Jay's top acts, was now Constellation's headline artist.

Gene's first Constellation singles were marginal successes. However, it wasn't long afterwards that Gene got right back in the rhythm and started racking up one hit after another. I was still producing him behind the scene, but Bunky continued to receive official credit because I was still working for Columbia and not allowed to moonlight. Curtis Mayfield continued to write most of Gene's Constellation singles. After "Think Nothing About It" did okay locally, and "Just Be True" was a national pop hit during the summer of '64, "Bless Our Love," written by Jerry Butler's younger brother Billy, did well for Gene that fall. However, the big year for Gene was 1965. He struck gold with a string of Mayfield compositions that I produced, which included: "What Now," "You Can't Hurt Me No More," "Gonna Be Good Times," and the biggest smash hit of these was "Nothing Can Stop Me," which hit number three on the R&B charts.

However, Gene came out with an unexpected hit that same year, recorded live in concert at the glorious Regal Theater in front of a packed ecstatic crowd. This recording was released under the name "Rainbow '65," the live version of Gene's 1963 hit. The live version turned out to be a greater seller than his studio rendition, soaring to #2 on national R&B charts.

I was there the night we recorded Gene's performance. It was absolutely electrifying. After the emcee introduced him, the music for "Rainbow" started playing, and the women in the audience went berserk. When Gene got to the part where he fell down to his knees, sweat was rolling down his face, and he started pleading, "Ba-by, ba-by, ba-by – ba-by, ba-by, ba-by." But when he said "please" in a long high note, women started falling out, and the place went bonkers. Gene was a consummate performer. This was a once in a lifetime performance on a magical night at the majestic Regal Theater. Curtis Mayfield himself could not have written that song with the level of intensity that Gene Chandler poured into it that night. It was fantastic. As a result of the phenomenal sensation of this record, we rode the wave of "Rainbow 65" success for weeks on end.

The Man Behind the Music

Not long after "Rainbow 65," another artist, Major Lance, was scheduled to record some Curtis Mayfield material. He was supposed to record the song "Nothing Can Stop Me." But I didn't feel that this song was really right for Major and I told Curtis as much. I told him not to give Major that song. During this same time, Curtis had another song entitled "The Monkey Time" that Gene was slated to record. However, when Gene went to Curtis about doing "The Monkey Time," Curtis informed Gene that he had made a promised to me to cut "Monkey Time" on Major Lance. So Gene came to me and said, "I gave up on doing 'Monkey Time' because he said you were gonna do it on Major. So now you've got to give me 'Nothing Can Stop Me.'" I quickly agreed to that because now we had the right songs for both artists.

After Gene went solo, we did our best to keep the Dukays going for a while. They got a new lead vocalist, Charles Davis. He was a very handsome young man with straight black hair, and he was an accomplished vocalist. Their first record with Charles singing lead, "Please Help," was written by Bernice Williams as an answer to the Tokens' "The Lion Sleeps Tonight." It was a local hit on Vee-Jay in 1962. But their next two singles didn't do anything, and the group fell apart after that. In a final hurrah, Bunky would produce a couple of solo records by Charles for Constellation. By then, the young singer had been renamed Nolan Chance. His "She's Gone" single was a regional hit in early '65. But neither the Dukays nor Nolan would record anything else that remotely resembled a hit. After that, Constellation, the once shining star label, sputtered out and folded.

Chapter 4

It wasn't long before the inevitable happened. As much as I tried to keep a low profile on my involvement with Gene Chandler's blockbuster hits, the word started to spread. Even though I tried to be as inconspicuous as possible, soon I was in the spotlight and my talent for producing had been illuminated for all to see. In June of 1962, the word got out that I was the actual producer of "Duke Of Earl" rather than Bunky. Therefore, I was called to New York to meet with David Kapralik, who was the director of the pop A&R department for both Columbia and its Epic subsidiary. To my surprise, I was given a promotion to become head of Columbia's newly created Chicago A&R office out of the CBS Building at 630 N. McClurg Court. This was a monumental move for both me and Columbia, because I would be the first black A&R executive in the entire CBS operation.

Dave told me, "You're going to be basically a general manager, which means that you're going to produce the records, mix them, and master them, and then you've got to go on the road and promote them. You'll have to do everything!" That was fine with me. I liked the fact that I would be involved in every aspect of the production process. This would also mean that I was in control and could basically write my own ticket.

The Man Behind the Music

David Kapralik wasn't your stereotypical Jewish guy with the yarmulke and all. He was of a short and thin stature, but had a very hip and cool demeanor. He used to hang out at all the hip places. He was always among the in-crowd wherever he went. He had a fabulous apartment that had a breathtaking view of Central Park, and he was debonair, always dressing very nicely. Dave could always get into those exclusive clubs and restaurants that were "reservation only." Even without a reservation, he had enough clout to get choice seats in these exclusive establishments. And he was known for always brandishing one of those thin cigars he loved to smoke. He knew how to stay on a person's good side, because he had a way of connecting with just about anyone. Whatever level you were on, he could go there with you. But as cordial a person as he was, he was a shrewd businessman and his temerity more than compensated for his small frame. He didn't take crap from anybody.

After meeting with David in New York, I returned to Chicago to start my new position. The CBS television studio was a huge facility. It was a former sports arena that had been converted into headquarters for CBS television in 1956. Its Studio 1 was the site of the famous 1960 debate between John F. Kennedy and Richard Nixon that helped get Kennedy elected President. After getting settled in on my first day there at CBS, I had to pick a secretary from a pool of administrative aides. The first one they sent to me was a very nice black young lady. Maybe they felt this was the appropriate thing to do because I was the only black executive. However, this young lady only worked for me a short time because she soon left to go off to college. Right before she got ready to leave, she made a recommendation for her replacement. She asked me if I would consider hiring Adrienne Lasker, a Jewish young lady who was just as sweet as she could be. She worked for me for the rest of the time that I was there.

My office was on the second floor and I had a rehearsal space upstairs that had another adjoining office close to the recording studio. The recording studio wasn't as big as Universal's facilities, but it was nice. Jim Felix was in charge of the studio, and he was an excellent engineer as well as.

By the time November 1963 rolled around, my production schedule was picking up and things were getting busy. However, on Friday, November 22nd, I was walking down the hall at CBS, when an ominous announcement

Carl H. Davis, Sr.

blared out over the P.A. system. President John F. Kennedy had been assassinated in Dallas, Texas. This was the most shocking news report that I had ever heard. If only for a brief moment in time, America seemed to stand still. It's a strange thing, but here it is almost fifty years later and people still ask, "Do you remember where you were when President Kennedy was killed?" I was at CBS in the hallway walking toward my office. It was a very sad day. Many were in tears, others glued to the television sets and radios trying to get the latest updates on this tragic moment in American history. The light spirited atmosphere normally associated with the end of the week, payday Friday, quickly gave way to a dark somber spirit of grief and sadness. As one could imagine, not much work got done the rest of that day – the infamous day that "Camelot" died.

Though I was headquartered in Chicago, some of my early productions for Columbia were recorded in other cities. I often traveled to places like New York, Los Angeles, and on several occasions Nashville, Tennessee. For one project, I went down to Nashville to produce a girl group called the Buttons. They had a local pop hit in 1962, a dance number called the "Shimmy Shimmy Watusi." I loved going to Nashville. It was a welcomed change of pace from the typical hustle and bustle of New York or Chicago. Nashville, like a beautiful southern belle, was elegant and graceful. Nashville had the Grand Ole Opry and Music Row, where many of the studios were located. I love country music and especially the sound of those steel and box guitars. Each song has a powerful storyline behind a soothing melody.

Nashville had several very chic recording studios. They had one studio that when you entered in, you had to walk down two levels. There, you saw a circular sunken area, where all the musicians played. It was shaped something like a big pit. That's where some of the hottest music in Nashville was being cut. Big name country celebrities who are now household names got their start as session musicians who played right in that very studio.

One of my next releases was a song called "The Bird," which was one of my Chicago productions. Richard Parker, the guy who wrote it, came to me with this out-of-sight dance tune that he sang with another guy named Jerry Brown. That's why they were called the Dutones, because they were a duo. "The Bird" did pretty well for them during the early weeks of 1963. Later on, Richard would be a songwriter for me at Brunswick.

I was the first producer to take future soul star Otis Clay into the stu-

The Man Behind the Music

dio in 1962 to do secular material. Up until that point, he only sang gospel music. However, for a reason that I still don't know until this day, Columbia never released his four sides. Otis went on to several other labels in his career and had some releases that did pretty well on the charts. However, some time after a long career in secular music, he returned to his gospel music roots.

Another entertainer who was assigned to me was a young man named Ted Taylor. Ted came from Los Angeles. Ted was a natural tenor, but his voice was so high that people often mistook his singing for a female vocalist. However, Ted had lots of feeling and plenty of soul. The sessions that I cut on him took place in both Chicago and Nashville, and were released on OKeh records, a subsidiary of Columbia Records. Ted had actually had a big record years before I cut him, "Be Ever Wonderful," so by that time, his artistry was established. We eventually formed a band, which included my brother Cliff on sax, where I believe Riley Hampton did the arrangements. We used to meet up at the Sutherland Lounge, where we had some very memorable rehearsals. Then we took him into Columbia Studios and cut some tunes on him that did pretty well. Ted wrote a lot of his own songs, like "Can't Take No More" and "Need You Home," which were songs on the album that I produced in 1963. It featured a remake of his former hit "Be Ever Wonderful."

I also had a brief stint as a gospel producer for a Columbia subsidiary, Epic Records, in mid-May of '63, where I recorded Bessie Griffin & the Gospel Pearls. Ironically, we did not record their music in a church or even in a recording studio, but in a Chicago nightclub. I had flown out to California and met with the whole group, and they were just a bunch of descent Christian women. I really can't recall why I was insensitive to the fact that these were religious people, but it probably stemmed from the reality that I wasn't a religious man myself. Maybe it was as Flip Wilson's character Geraldine used to say: "The devil made me do it." But as it turned out, I arranged for the session to be recorded at a nightclub called The Bear. However, the departure from the normal liturgical setting that they would have been more accustomed to did not have any impact on them in this contrasting den-of-sin environment. They were not affected at all. Their soulful songs of inspiration translated onto wax just fine, in what others may have considered contrary conditions. In the end, the album did well. I also believe that God must have smiled on this project, because I ended up receiving a Grammy nomination for that album.

There were some other memorable assignments that I received there at CBS, some more risky than others. However, one comes to mind which I ended up not even producing. There was this flirtatious 17 or 18 year old Italian girl who they assigned to me. She was an ex-Mouseketeer. The young lady only had marginal musical talent, but I tried anyway to get something done with her. The real problem was that she had the hots for me and wanted to get me in the sack. I was terrified, because I could see the headlines the next day: "A&R exec for Columbia Records caught with a teenaged Mouseketeer!" That was it. I was through with her. After I saw what was really going on, I made it clear to everyone that I couldn't work with her any longer. Eventually, they reassigned her to Abner and Bunky. They didn't have any reservations about accommodating this promiscuous young lady's special needs. Though it was none of my business what they did with her, it's safe to assume that not all their sessions occurred in a recording studio.

After a string of lesser known artists, one of my first major discoveries while working at CBS was Walter Jackson, who remains my favorite singer to this day. Walter was born in Pensacola, Florida, but was raised in the ghettos of Detroit, Michigan. A serious bout with polio during his childhood left him on crutches for the rest of his life. Polio may have taken the use of his legs, but it couldn't cripple his golden vocal chords or his determined spirit. Walter had already earned a reputation as an up and coming vocalist on the club circuit in Detroit. Though his specialty was singing pop standards, Walter had the versatility to perform a wide range of music, including commercial R&B hits.

My discovery of Walter Jackson came out of a relationship I had with a young lady named Marion "Skippy" Crawford. When Granny and I used to go to Detroit to promote records, we used to stay at a hotel that was popular with many of the black entertainers and those in the music business. Whenever we stayed there, we would always have a ball. We'd dance, have a few drinks and play bid whist and poker till the wee hours of the morning. Personalities like Aretha Franklin and her future husband at the time, Ted White, would be there, too. I liked playing against Ted, because I'd whip his butt in bid whist and take some of his money. Aretha couldn't stand to see me beating her fiancé. She used to get mad, complaining, "You know you just cheatin' Carl!" I'd quickly retort by saying, "And you know you just drunk, too!" We weren't really mad with each other. It was all in the context of having fun.

Aretha and I grew to be very close. She and Ted actually wanted me to produce some of her records. So they asked John Hammond, the head of the A&R department, if I could produce her. But he said no for personal reasons, because he actually wanted to produce her himself. Regardless, Aretha and I always maintained a great rapport, back then and even to this very day.

One night while we were staying at the hotel, I was introduced to Skippy, and we hit it off real well. One day after returning to Chicago, I got a call from Skippy. She was excited about this vocalist she had just seen in Detroit. "Carl, you've got to come hear this guy singing over here!" The first thing that came to my mind was, "If he's so good, why hasn't Motown snatched him up yet?" So that's what I asked her, and she said, "He did go over to Motown, but they wanted him to sing with some group, and he didn't want to sing with a group." Since I was planning another trip back to Detroit soon anyway, I decided to come see Walter Jackson for myself.

A short time later, I returned to Detroit to finally see Walter Jackson. Skippy picked me up at the airport. We went to this club where he was performing. I was sitting there waiting for this artist to come on, and they started playing the music to "That Old Black Magic." This guy on crutches came out of a door behind the stage. You could tell he had braces on his legs, even though you couldn't see them. I just knew that he couldn't be the guy that I came here to see. So I'm still waiting to see who was coming out. Then the guy on crutches came right to the forefront of the stage and grabbed the microphone. The next thing I know, he started singing "That Old Black Magic" in the richest baritone voice that I had ever heard. I was blown away and I was sold right there on the spot. I thought, "My God, how could somebody not do something with this voice?" The beauty of his voice completely overshadowed his physical disability, and I didn't even see the crutches anymore after he started singing. After hearing him, I was glad that Motown didn't do anything with him. After the show, Walter came over to the table and introduced himself. I asked him, "What do you think about coming to Chicago?" He said, "Fine with me. I'm ready to go!" And that was the beginning of our long relationship.

Back in Chicago, a friend of mine managed some apartment build-

Carl H. Davis, Sr.

ings and I called him to see if I could get Walter a place to stay. My contact recommended an apartment for him in this two-flat building right on 83rd and South Park. This was a convenient location and right across the street from a Jewel food store. I went there to look at the apartment and I made sure it was a first floor apartment, or that there was at least an elevator. It turned out to be a nice two-bedroom first floor apartment.

Walter came to Chicago, and we got him some furniture and set him up in this apartment. I paid the rent, and then I started working with him on some songs. I sent the word out to all the big publishing houses about Walter Jackson. In the beginning, the publishers were slow to respond, and getting someone interested was a bit like pulling teeth. But that all changed as soon as we went in the studio and recorded Walter. After, that I didn't have any more trouble getting songs. Everybody was sending us stuff then.

Walter's first single, which I co-wrote with Detroit songwriter Richard "Popcorn" Wylie, was titled "This World Of Mine." It came out on Columbia in the late summer of 1962. Walter followed it with two more 45's on Columbia, but it would be another couple of years before he started scoring consistent hits. Curtis Mayfield wrote Walter's first OKeh single, "That's What Mama Say." But to be honest, I didn't want him to do any of Curtis' songs. I really wanted Walter to be more of a Billy Eckstine styled singer. Besides, Walter was not all that impressed with Curtis Mayfield like everybody else was. Since Walter and I saw eye-to-eye, he was more apt to follow my lead as opposed to Curtis Mayfield's. If I liked something, he would like it. If I didn't like it, he didn't like it. He used to call me off to the side and say, "Carl, I know Curtis is great and all that, but I don't want him producing me."

In August 1964, I produced Walter, who did another Curtis Mayfield song titled "It's All Over." This time, his release made some national rumbling. From then on, whenever I did the producing on Walter and Curtis wrote the songs, I made sure that the label read "Produced by Carl Davis and Curtis Mayfield," because I thought that gave Curtis additional credibility for his work. It also made the label and the music more marketable to have both our names on there. The B-side of the record was a swinger that Aretha sent him called, "Lee Cross."

Walter had two big R&B hits for OKeh in 1965, "Suddenly I'm All Alone" and "Welcome Home." Both were ballads, and the first one was written by Van McCoy. Van and I were tight, too. He wrote a couple of songs for me when I first started over at Columbia. Van was a young, thin guy – really nice. We didn't spend a lot of time together, but whatever we did, we enjoyed it. He was a hell of a songwriter. "Welcome Home" was written by Chip Taylor, the same guy who wrote "Wild Thing."

I produced Walter's second OKeh album and had him do several standards: "My Funny Valentine," "Moon River," and "Moonlight In Vermont." That was the kind of stuff that I liked to do on Walter. My arranger, Riley Hampton, used to love to do those kind of songs. I liked Riley because he did Jerry Butler's "Moon River" for Vee-Jay, and I just loved that arrangement. Riley also arranged a lot of Etta James' early '60s classics for Chess, including "At Last."

Riley was the kind of arranger that if you had six strings, he would write a different part for each string. Most arrangers would take one part and have each one of them harmonize, but they'd all be playing the same thing. That wasn't good enough for Riley. He had each violin playing a different part, but they all complemented each other. The result was so dynamic, and it just sounded so huge. When I multi'd them, which was a little engineering technique where we would dub duplicate tracks on top of one another, it sounded like you had an entire symphony orchestra in there. Those are the kinds of beautiful sounds that I would prefer to use for my recordings. Unfortunately, the big orchestration sounds weren't the ones that were commercial hits. So we were forced to go back to typical R&B arrangements that could sell units and produce revenue.

In the spring of 1963, Kapralik promoted me again, this time to A&R manager of OKeh Records. OKeh was a legendary label founded by Otto K. E. Heinemann in the early 1900s. The name OKeh came from the initials of his name. During the '50s, as Columbia's R&B subsidiary, OKeh had been home to some great performers like the Treniers, Chuck Willis, Big Maybelle, and others. But now, artist development and production for OKeh was my responsibility.

No matter how much effort you put into developing an artist, there were still these nagging ex-factors. Trying to gauge what songs and which artists would be a commercial success can be difficult to predict at times. During my stay at OKeh, I worked with a few artists, but my top-selling artist at OKeh would turn out to be Major Lance. He was born in Winterville,

Carl H. Davis, Sr.

Mississippi but grew up on Chicago's Westside. He then lived in the near Northside Cabrini-Green housing projects, where he went to Wells Community Academy High School with Jerry Butler and Curtis Mayfield. Ironically, Major was not a nickname. It actually was his first name.

Before Major was involved in the music business, he took up boxing for a while and also sang with a local gospel group called the Five Gospel Harmonaires. He then sang with a local group called the Floats, but they never recorded any material. He'd had a single out called "I Got a Girl" on Mercury back in 1959, that was written and produced by his friend Curtis Mayfield, but it was a flop. After that, Major worked odd jobs here and there and was working at a drugstore by Cabrini-Green when he came over to me. Calvin Carter at Vee-Jay Records couldn't do anything with him and didn't want him anymore. So to get rid of him, Calvin sent him to me and I'm so glad that he did. When I heard Major sing, I could hear a unique sound in his voice. My gut feeling was that Calvin sent over a diamond in the rough. All Major needed was the right person to believe in him and develop him. He wasn't getting that type of attention over there at Vee-Jay, so he came to me, where I turned him into a hit maker.

I must admit that Major wore me down in the beginning. He used to come by my office every day, rain or shine. He knew that I liked coffee, so he'd run out and get me cups of coffee. Every five minutes, he would run out and get me another cup. It got to the point where either I had to keep him busy in the studio, or have a stroke from a caffeine overdose. But he meant well. He only wanted to please me because he knew that I was his best chance at becoming a success.

In September of '62, Major came to me with a song that was written by Curtis called "Delilah." We cut it on him, not long after I arrived at CBS. It wasn't a very big record, but it was enough to make people begin to pay attention to who Major Lance was.

I knew Curtis had a lot of material, but not everything that he had was right for Major. So I used to go to Curtis' house out in Markham, which is a small town in the south suburbs of Chicago. I was amazed. The great songwriting genius Curtis Mayfield used to have all his songs on cassette tapes that he kept in bushel baskets. In most cases, he only had maybe three or four bars of every song. Whenever he'd come up with another hook or melody, he'd record three or four bars of it with guitar accompaniment. He'd stop and throw it into the bushel basket, then put a new tape in to be ready to record a new song. I guess he did it that way so he wouldn't forget any new inspirations when they came to him.

Curtis Mayfield was something else. Every time I used to listen to his material to find the right songs for Major, if I said, "Man, I like that one," he would pick up on it and say that he was already going to use that one for the Impressions. After a while, I got wise to his little game. So I'd listen to all of the songs, and when it was over he'd ask,

"Which one do you like?"

With a big smile on my face, I would reply, "I like all of 'em! Which ones are you not going to do on the group?"

And he said, "Well, I know we're not gonna do 'The Monkey Time' because that's a dance tune, and Fred and Sam (Fred Cash and Sam Gooden, the other Impressions) don't want to do dance tunes."

I said, "Okay, well, give me that one. I'll take that one."

Of course, that's the one I wanted in the first place! But with Curtis, that's the game you had to play. As brilliant as he was, he couldn't decide for himself which were the best of his songs, so he needed me as a sounding board. Curtis trusted my judgment. He knew that I had a good ear for songs that had potential to be commercial successes.

Now that I had the song that I wanted, it needed a fresh arrangement that suited Major's style. So I went to see my arranger Johnny Pate, and there at his house, I hummed out all of the parts, and Johnny got it all on tape. However, I gave him the freedom to do what he wanted to do with the horns. As a result of the collaboration between the three of us (myself, Johnny Pate and Curtis Mayfield), we created a very hip sound. That unique blend of the horns and rhythm section, Curtis Mayfield's writing, my producing, and Johnny's arrangements, became known as what was later called the "Chicago Sound." Johnny was able to put down the kind of arrangements that no one else was doing. That's what made us better. That's what made us unique. That's what made the Chicago Sound.

Back in those days, we used to call those arrangers "putter-downers," because if you couldn't read and write music, you didn't know how to accurately express what you had in mind musically. So I would go out there to Johnny's and say, "Let's start with the drums," or I would say, "John, I hear this for the bass line." If it was a Curtis Mayfield song and he would be playing the guitar, I would say, "I need the horns to complement Curtis' guitar," and he would then compose all of that. I always tried to ensure that I had my own sound. We had so much success with it, Curtis went and got Johnny for his own material with the Impressions. So we both had a very similar sound.

We decided collectively to try to do something different than other labels, using prominent trombones and trumpets to make the Chicago sound distinguishable so you could recognize it. Motown had their own sound. Stax had their own sound. Los Angeles, New York and Philadelphia all had their own sounds. We purposed not to be like any of them, so we assembled a house band for my OKeh productions, who captured and mastered our distinctive sound. When it came to the auditioning and hiring of the musicians, I left that up to my brother Cliff, because he knew all of the musicians anyway.

My usual trombonists were Morris Ellis and John Avant, and the trumpeters were Maury Watson and Paul Serrano. I primarily used John Young and Floyd Morris, jazz-trained piano players. We always hired Louis Satterfield on bass, and either Al Duncan or Maurice White would be on drums. Maurice White was a great percussionist who went on to form the mega-group Earth, Wind & Fire. Phil Upchurch, Gerald Sims, and Kermit Chandler were among my frequent session guitarists, and Bobby Christian was my main percussionist. He could play vibes, castanets, even some guitar. One of my signature arrangements was that I always liked my records to end on the title of the song. In most cases, the vamp is pretty much the chorus anyway, so we would end the songs there and then fade it out.

When we got ready to go into the studio to do "The Monkey Time" with Major, I asked Curtis if the Impressions could do the vocal background, and if he could play guitar, because his sound and the chords he used were different. Curtis tuned his guitar to the black keys of the piano, which means that all his open strings were sharps instead of natural notes. As a result, all his chords and his riffs sounded different. That was the main contributing factor to his unique sound, coupled with his having his own way of playing the guitar.

"The Monkey Time" blasted off to number eight on the pop charts and number two on the R&B charts. National sales of the record catapulted it to gold soon after its release during the summer of 1963. Calvin Carter, over at Vee-Jay, who called himself getting rid of Major, was blown away by Major's tremendous success with us over at OKeh. When I first heard "The Monkey Time" at Curtis' house, I knew this was going to be a hit. Sarcastically, I've always boasted that even I could have sang lead on "The Monkey Time," and it still would have been a smash. The fact is, no matter who recorded it, it would have been a hit.

Before the year was over, Major had an encore hit with another of Curtis' compositions, "Hey Little Girl." It was a follow-up to "The Monkey Time." In those days, if you had a hit, you had to come back with a follow-up that tended to have the same feel. The musical arrangements were almost identical, with just minor adjustments to accommodate the lyrics, but the vamp was the same. By the time Major recorded "Hey Little Girl," Sam and Fred of the Impressions were not too keen about being anyone else's background singers. To them, I guess it seemed to be a step backwards, because they already were well known by this time.

Another of Major's huge sellers was Curtis' mystical "Um, Um, Um, Um, Um, Um," which was a number five pop smash at the beginning of 1964. There's an interesting story behind how this song came about. The song that we ended up releasing wasn't actually what Curtis had written. Originally, the song was rather nebulous and mystical, and it didn't have an ending. Curtis' concept for the song was reminiscent of the Sirens, the mythological goddesses who called out in song to sailors passing by their island. Their enchanting song was so beautifully irresistible that sailors would change course and head for the island, then be destroyed by the deadly reefs. That was the concept in which the song was originally conceived – a mystical calling.

I went to Curtis and told him that the song was great, but that he needed to change it around so that it talks about a female, love, or something like that. In those days, if it wasn't a dance song, it had to be a love song. With that, he reconsidered and changed the lyrics, even though it didn't really turn out to be a love song.

There were times that I co-wrote songs with Curtis, but he would never share any of the writing credits with me or anyone else. Because of that, he never shared any of the revenues with me either. That's something that Curtis just wouldn't do. In hindsight, I see that it was a smart thing to do. He wouldn't give up any of his publishing or writing credits. If you worked with Curtis, you had to do things his way.

After we started having all this success, I asked Curtis, "Why don't you come work for me? You can still go on the road with the Impressions, but when you come back, Monday through Thursday, you could work for me as my assistant." He liked that idea, so I hired him as my assistant producer. My office was huge, so he shared my office and I went out and bought him his own desk. I think he liked the feel of being a producer with an office.

Major had been managed by Otis Leavill, who worked at the same drugstore as Major did and was also a member of the R&B group the Floats. They had a longstanding relationship and Major trusted him because they were really close. Otis had come to Chicago from his Georgia hometown when he was two. He'd started out singing gospel with his family's Cobb Quartet before joining Major in the Floats. Otis also wrote "I'm A Soldier Boy" for Dee Clark. When Major originally came in to see me, Otis was with him and from then on, they always came to my office together. One thing that I noticed about Otis was, he had a great ear for talent. So I made him an offer to come work for me as a talent scout, and he readily agreed.

As it turned out, for ninety percent of the artists that I produced, Otis was the one who went out and found them and brought them to me. He didn't want to produce them, but he had a good enough ear to say that this is going to be a good act. Otis wanted to be a singer. However, I didn't particularly like him as a singer because at that time, he was singing in that falsetto voice the way Curtis did. So he asked me to produce his record entitled "Let Her Love Me," which was a national R&B hit in 1965, on the Mercury label. But much more than an artist and my right hand man, he turned out to be my best friend. Our relationship went far beyond the music business.

Major kept on making hits for me through 1964, including the Latin-tinged "The Matador." I wrote it with him and Billy Butler, who took over the guitar duties from Curtis and sang the background with his group. Major invented the dance that went with the song, inspired by the way matadors stuck their lances into the bulls. That's the way the dance went – he stuck out one arm as part of the dance. It was pretty reflective of the matador's moves. Major was a great dancer because at one time he was training to be a boxer, so he'd use those boxing moves in his dance routes.

Major's next hits were "It Ain't No Use" and "Girls," as well as the pop hit "Rhythm" later that year, all of which were written by Curtis. On

The Man Behind the Music

some of the tunes Curtis wrote, like "Rhythm," he didn't have the same concept for the song that I did. I was feeling more of a calypso or Latin kind of rhythm, so I had them add that to the songs. Curtis also penned Major's first three hits of 1965: "Sometimes I Wonder," "Come See," and "Ain't It A Shame." Another of my main session guitarists, Gerald Sims, came up with Lance's last hit of the year, "Too Hot To Hold," which he co-produced with me.

It didn't take long for word to get around Chicago that if you wanted to make it in the music business, you needed to get in with Carl Davis. Seemed like everybody at Chess wanted to come over to me. But I didn't want that. I wanted to pick my own people. I didn't want anybody who had already been influenced by another label's sound. I certainly didn't want to have to reprogram anybody. I wanted to be totally different. When somebody heard one of our records, I wanted them to say, "That's a Carl Davis record!" or "That's the Chicago Sound!"

Gerald Sims was one of the musicians who helped consolidate our unique sound. Though he was a good guitar player, he was known to make mistakes during the sessions. A foul note never got by me. I may not be able to read a note of music, but there wasn't anything off about my hearing. I could hear a rat piss on cotton, so if you made a mistake, I'd be on that intercom speaker in a hot second, saying, "Hold up, we have to do that again!" When necessary, we would do tracks over and over again, until we got them right. All the other musicians would get pissed off, because they wouldn't be making any mistakes. But I liked Gerald. That's why I continued working with him. Overall, he was a good musician who we never had too many problems with. Gerald also had two '63 OKeh singles of his own, so he was both player and product.

Another person who came to me through Otis was Billy Butler, who was Jerry Butler's younger brother. He had a vocal group called the Enchanters, originally consisting of tenors Errol Batts and John Jordan, baritone Jesse Tillman, and bass Alton Howell. However, for the first couple of OKeh sessions, the group was down to just Batts and Tillman. Otis informed me that nobody would sign Billy because of Jerry. So I signed him and the group to OKeh. He needed some equipment, so we bought him a guitar and an amp that he would leave at the office.

I think what set Billy apart from other people was not so much his singing, but that he was a disciple of Curtis Mayfield. I really thought that he could be the closest thing to Curtis. He used to tune his guitar similar to the way that Curtis did. Billy just copied that. If you couldn't get Curtis Mayfield for a session, then you would go find Billy, because he could play the chords close to the way Curtis would. And besides that, he was a heck of a songwriter. There were a lot of songs that we did on Major that Billy wrote. Billy's writing style was very similar to Curtis'.

Johnny Pate arranged Billy's group's 1963 debut single "Found True Love," which Billy wrote with Curtis. The Enchanters did a little bit better their next time out with Curtis' "Gotta Get Away," and in '65 they scored a number six national R&B seller with Mayfield's "I Can't Work No Longer." For that song, we cut the music tracks in New York with Teacho Wiltshire providing the arrangements, and the vocals were added in Chicago. But not too long after that release, the Enchanters broke up. So Billy released a solo on OKeh which was a hit in '66, entitled "Right Track," arranged by Gerald Sims.

It was normally against my policy for one person's name to be out in front because of all the strife it can cause within the group. But in Billy's case, we were trying to capitalize on the fact that he was Jerry Butler's brother. In the beginning, the rest of the group didn't seem to mind being called Billy Butler & the Enchanters. But after awhile, that got old, and they resented the fact that Billy was getting all the exposure. Before we released their last record, we seriously considered just putting his name on all their records, and that's exactly what we did with "Right Track." I liked Billy. He was a good young man. He was serious about his career and was always amenable to whatever needed to be done.

Another brilliant group that was brought to me – probably the best vocal group that I ever had – was the Artistics. When Major Lance first introduced me to the Artistics, Robert Dobyne was their lead singer. The rest of the Westside-based group consisted of first tenor Larry Johnson, second tenor Jesse Bolian, and baritone/bass Aaron Floyd. Even though I made a concerted effort to maintain our unique Chicago sound, the Artistics would be a departure from that formula. I loved the Motown sound, and when it came to the Artistics' OKeh releases, I wanted to capture a sound similar to that of the Temptations. Robert was a hell of a singer, but he was only featured on the Artistics' 1963 debut, "I Need Your Love." After Charles Davis, formerly of the Dukays, briefly replaced Dobyne, their sound was missing something. So I, let's say, convinced, former El Dorado singer Marvin Smith to come in and take over as lead singer. Initially, Marvin did not want to be in the group. After already singing with the El Dorados, Marvin had his sights on a solo career. But I told him that I could not accommodate his aspirations because I didn't have any open spots for a solo artist. In saying that, I basically left him no choice but to sing lead for the Artistics. It was a ballsy move on my part, but it was my call to make. It wasn't just about what he wanted; it was about the betterment of the group. Besides, I felt strongly that he was the missing link that the group needed.

With a new lead singer in place, we had the Artistics do a remake of Marvin Gaye's Motown recording "Get My Hands On Some Lovin," which was a local hit in 1964. Then at the end of '65, their follow-up release "This Heart Of Mine" started to climb on the national R&B charts. We did well with "This Heart Of Mine," which was written by Barrett Strong, Norman Whitfield's future songwriting partner at Motown. There was even more Motown talent involved in this project. The arrangement was done by William "Sonny" Sanders, who had been with Motown during its early days. He had sung with the Satintones, one of Motown's earliest vocal groups. Sonny called me and told me that he and Berry Gordy fell out, and that he was no longer with Motown. I told him not to worry about it and if he came to Chicago, I would put him up at my apartment at Marina City. I let him stay there until he found a place of his own. Sonny and I were very close. He knew all of the Funk Brothers, Motown's house band, including their bassist James Jamerson. Sonny was responsible for getting them to Chicago to work with me in the studio.

Right around this same period, I was also producing a girl group called the Opals. I was always a little leery of girl groups, especially after that episode with the Starlets and "I Sold My Heart To The Junkman." But the Opals were special, and their sound was fresh. The Opals were Rosie "Tootsie" Addison, Myra Tillotson, Juanita Tucker, and Rose E. Kelly, who sang lead. They were from East Chicago, Indiana, and they were all really nice kids. Mickey McGill of the Dells sent them over to me. I was very close with the Dells at the time, even though I wasn't producing them back in those days. So the Opals came down to the studio, and we started them out doing background vocals for several of our artists, like Major Lance and

Carl H. Davis, Sr.

Otis Leavil. They also sang behind Betty Everett on her smash "It's In His Kiss (The Shoop Shoop Song)" that Calvin Carter produced over at Vee-Jay. In October of 1963, they earned their chance for us to do something on them.

In 1963, their debut releases on OKeh were two of my brother Clifford's songs, "Losers Weepers," and "Take It Right." The latter was co-written with Phil Upchurch. However, the Opals were better known for their follow-up singles, "Does It Matter," written by Billy Butler, and "You Can't Hurt Me No More," written by Curtis Mayfield, which Gene Chandler would make into a hit the next year on Constellation. Another Mayfield song, "I'm So Afraid," was the Opals' last OKeh single in 1965. Unfortunately, the Opals never had a national hit, nor did they ever get the recognition that I felt they deserved. They were respectful young ladies and very good friends to both me and my wife. During the time that they were working on their project, they actually moved in with us at our house at 87th and Calumet to avoid the commute from East Chicago, Indiana. They stayed with us for two or three months, and we all got along just fine.

I was blessed to have a wife who didn't mind a lot of company. Just about all the acts starring at the Regal came out to my house on 87th Street. I had a pool table, and we shot pool there. Along with groups like the Vibrations, Dionne Warwick came by, and so did E. Rodney Jones, program director and deejay at WVON-AM, which was Chicago's leading R&B radio station and which was owned by the Chess brothers. On holidays like the Fourth of July, I would get the Artistics. We would open up my garage, and they'd set up the band in there. We'd have us a ball. E. Rodney became one of my best friends. He would start playing one of my records early in the morning, and by 6 p.m. that evening, I would already have gotten calls from the local stores with big orders for the record. Rodney could bust a record wide open all by himself, or let you know that you didn't have anything. The years that we spent on 87th street are certainly among some of my fondest memories – I will always cherish those days.

Another artist that CBS assigned to me who was a real firecracker was Little Richard. It was out in California where I worked with him. We had a few rehearsal sessions, but nothing of any substance or significance ever resulted from my involvement with him. Personally, I didn't care too much for Little Richard. It wasn't his flamboyant risqué demeanor (that some found to be troubling and others thought was amusing), but he didn't have

The Man Behind the Music

the vocal quality that I like in a singer. Though he had a controversial look, he was professional. He listened and I never had any problems with him. However, he was not somebody who I would have signed. Besides, we were trying to get away from the "Good Golly Miss Molly" sound, and trying to get him to sing something of some substance. I preferred to work with artists who relied on true vocal abilities, not all that yelling and screaming gimmicky stuff. Not to knock Little Richard in any way; his look and his vocal style have made him a legend. However, my disinterest in him boiled down to my own personal preferences.

Another very controversial personality that I worked with, who was not as flamboyant as he was outspoken, was the world heavyweight boxing champion, Cassius Clay. One time I brought Cassius into a New York studio, along with his close friend, singer songwriter Sam Cooke. I had already met Sam on the Chicago music scene a couple of times. We used to run into each other because we were both involved in producing. However, we really became tight after we collaborated together on a production with his friend Cassius Clay.

Cassius and Dave Kapralik had a good relationship, and Dave took me up to one of his camps in upstate New York, where Cassius was training for an upcoming fight with Sonny Liston. When we arrived, Cassius was in the midst of training with one of his sparring partners. When Cassius was finished, his playful mischievous side would come out. Cassius loved to mess with you. He'd be bobbing and weaving, throwing jabs at you, and making funny faces and stuff. That's just how Cassius was, the fun loving jovial type. After Dave introduced us, he asked me if I would do a session with Cassius. Cassius was excited about the whole idea and said, "Man, I want to do the Ben E. King song, 'Stand By Me.'" So I said okay.

When we started production, we got a copy of "Stand By Me" and we worked on finding the right key for him. I told Cassius, "I don't want you to get too comfortable. We'll get you a key that you've got to reach out for!" So after we found the right key, Horace Ott did the arrangement. Sam Cooke was out in the studio with him, coaching him on how to lay down vocals. Sam also did some background vocals as well. It was a great collaborative effort, and when it was finished, we had a good record on our hands. But soon after that, everything changed.

After winning a decisive battle over Sonny Liston, Cassuis Clay blew the lid off of the boxing world when he announced his conversion to Islam and his association with The Nation of Islam. Prior to the fight, reports had already been circulating about Clay's involvement with Malcolm X. These rumors of a Clay and Malcolm X association almost made the promoters call off the fight with Liston. So Clay agreed to make the announcement after the fight. However, once Clay made the announcement that he had become a Black Muslim, Columbia Records halted the project dead in its tracks, and refused to promote it any further. With that one move, Cassuis Clay's music career suffered a decisive knockout punch.

Before all this conversion stuff happened with Clay, he really liked girls. He used to have the photographer who ran around with him get him all kinds of women. But having said that, I never saw him do anybody any harm. He was a nice guy, not the mean abusive type. When he converted to Islam, all that changed. If he didn't know you, he didn't want you around. He was not as trusting and open as he was prior to his conversion. But even after all that, I still used to go up to his training camp when he was training for the rematch with that big ugly guy, Sonny Liston. Conversion or not, he still used to do outrageous stuff like drive his bus up on Sonny's lawn and taunt him. He was an expert at creating hype and he knew how to promote a fight.

Cassius was living on the Southside of Chicago, around 83rd Street, where he had a nice home. At that time, he was married to Sonja Clay, who used to sing at the Sutherland Lounge. She was just too worldly for him after he became a Muslim. She was a beautiful young lady. She didn't want to live by some strict moral code, being told that she couldn't wear lipstick and had to wear head coverings and long dresses. So they soon split up. Ali tended to be very fervent in his new found faith. On one occasion, he came by my house, went into the refrigerator, and started throwing all the pork products in the garbage can, claiming that swine meat was poison! Well I certainly did not agree with him on that, but I wasn't about to stop him either. I think I liked him better as Cassius Clay, but he is my friend and I still like him as Muhammad Ali, too.

One day when I was in my McClurg Court office, Bruce Roberts, the sports anchor at WBBM-TV, whose studios were in the same building, came to see me. I guess somebody had told him that I was friends with Cassius. Everybody had been trying to get an interview with him, but he wasn't granting any. Bruce said, "If you get me an interview with Muhammad Ali, I'll get you closed circuit television for your office. You can watch all the Bears games!" At that time, you couldn't watch the Bears when they played at home because they were blacked out locally by the NFL. So I agreed. I asked Cassius about doing an interview with Bruce, and he said, "I'll do it for you!" When he came to the studio to do the interview, he was in rare form. Ali shadowboxed all over the studio and down the hallways, everywhere. He was something else. I couldn't control Ali's antics in the studio, but Bruce was happy, and I got my closed-circuit television hook-up.

Chapter 5

Another artist that I worked with over the years was Mary Wells. Mary gained international fame at Motown Records with her hits "The One Who Really Loves You," "Two Lovers," and "My Guy." In 1964, when she reached the age of 21, she dissolved her contract with Berry Gordy and Motown. She happened to be close friends with Gene Chandler because he was dating Mary's road manager, May Hampton, while they were in New York performing together. Gene called and informed me that Mary believed Berry Gordy had blacklisted her because she had the audacity to walk away from Motown. Producers were refusing to work with her. Although she had made a few minor hits for 20th Century Fox right after she left, they weren't near as successful as her Motown hits. In November of 1965, Gene asked me if I would produce her as a favor to him, and I agreed to do a little moonlighting on her behalf.

I first met Mary at her apartment on Park Avenue in New York and we immediately formed an alliance. Gerald Sims and I sat down and wrote a song for her called "Dear Lover," that was similar to the pop standard "Hello Young Lovers." We slightly rearranged the opening melody and then we went into "Dear Lover" with an R&B grove as opposed to the big band jazz sound that others were doing with "Hello Young Lovers." I guess today we probably would have heard from the publishing company because the premise is similar, but they really are very different sounding songs. Back in those days, I think you could use four bars or something like that without having to pay.

In trying to create new material for her, we listened to a lot of her old songs to come up with a sound that had the same kind of groove that Motown had. I wrote the lyrics and Gerald did the melody, and vice versa. Then we had the Funk Brothers come down to Chicago from Motown over the weekend, and we had them cut the rhythm track. Sonny Sanders did the arrangement. We tried to make the record sound as close to Motown as we could. Atco Records, Atlantic's sister label, picked up "Dear Lover," and in early 1966, it became Mary's biggest hit since "My Guy."

At the time, Mary was living on Park Avenue in an upscale residential building. Her apartment was laid with chic décor coordinated in purple and white. Everything was just so elegant and nice. She had a beautiful white Afghan Hound. When you walked into her pad, the foyer was white marble, which led into a fabulous living room with stylish furniture and paintings on the walls. The walls were like a royal purple and the floor was covered with beautiful white carpeting. It was so luxurious, and fit for a queen.

Our relationship started out platonically, but at some point the sparks of romance quickly ignited. Maybe it was because Mabel and I were on hiatus at the time because of something stupid that I had probably done. I even temporarily moved into the apartment I had in Marina City. Yet, the separation from my wife apparently served as an unspoken reason for my brief fling with Mary. So a romance between us began that did not last very long.

Back in Chicago, Gene Chandler had brought in a group called the Peaches for me to produce. I think they were up there rehearsing one day, when Mary Wells came up the stairs to visit me in my office, looking as good as can be, with her long pretty hair. When she saw the Peaches, she immediately got jealous and lit into those young girls. She started fussing at them, saying, "I don't want any of you all flirting with my man, because you all can't afford him!" Then she started bossing them around, telling them what they could do, and what they couldn't do. That's when I had to step in and tell Mary about herself, which was one of our first blowouts. Ironically, I did end up marrying one of the Peaches. But that was long after Mary and

Carl H. Davis, Sr.

I split up.

Another confrontational incident between Mary and I that turned out to be the last straw occurred in Los Angles. We went out there to promote Major Lance on Shindig!, a weekly rock and roll program broadcast nationally on ABC-TV. There was a promotion woman out there who worked for Columbia. When I got there, they sent her over to my hotel to map out a plan of what we were going to do for Major. She was a really nice lady and quite professional, but she just wasn't my type.

However, Mary's over possessiveness and jealous personality kicked in and she assumed that I had some kind of relationship going with the promotions woman. That started a big argument between us. That's when I saw another side of Mary Wells. She became so enraged that she picked up a glass, broke it, and attempted to cut me with the jagged glass. That was the last straw. I was through with Mary Wells. I immediately had my room changed. It was a nice exclusive hotel and I told the guy at the front desk, "I don't care what she says, do not tell her where I am!" After she calmed down and realized what she had done, she was running around the hotel hollering, "Carl! Carl, come back baby. I'm sorry!" Needless to say, she did not get a second chance.

Life is full of swift transition. When one door closes, another door of opportunity often opens. All it takes is for one key element to be changed and the whole dynamic can be adversely affected. By the close of 1965, my tenure at CBS was near an end. The hits I produced for CBS and their subsidiary OKeh didn't make a difference. My relationship with CBS ran afoul after Dave Kapralik had been slapped with lawsuits from some of his dealings at the company. OKeh had been placed under the control of Len Levy – somebody I couldn't get along with to save my life. This man was a serious weed up my ass. We'd go to New York for A&R meetings, and whenever Levy would speak to me, it took everything in me to contain myself. This man had such an idiotic concept of how to develop new artists. His method was to point out whoever was hot at the time and copy that artist. For example, if Chuck Jackson was hot, then he would want me to get somebody that sounded like Chuck Jackson. If the Temptations were hot, he'd tell me to get somebody like the Temptations. I tried my best to reason with him. I said:

"You know, Len, I understand where you're coming from, but I'm trying to create my own sound. I don't want to copy somebody else's sound. I want somebody copying my sound. I'm trying to develop the Chicago sound."

"Well, we're not a Chicago label," he said with an attitude. "We're a national label, so we need a national sound."

I responded with an attitude, "I disagree with that. There's a distinct New York sound. You can tell New York from Motown. You can tell the California sound. I want to develop the Chicago sound."

So that was the gist of our initial problem. Besides, I thought by the time he took over, I had proven that I knew what the hell I was doing. So that's where the rift between us began, but little did I know at the time, there would be plenty more fuel to be thrown on this fire.

A short time had passed when the famous New York gossip columnist Walter Winchell printed an article in the paper stating, "Mary Wells and OKeh Records President, Carl Davis, were having an affair." I don't believe anyone in New York actually saw me with Mary. I think he was saying the rumor was that she was dating me. The column never stated definitively that we had been seen together or anything like that. Besides, during that specific time that Winchell was talking about, we weren't dating yet anyway, but we were involved in recording "Dear Lover."

Levy was livid. He directed me to return to New York so he could call me on the carpet in person. I didn't have a problem with that because I needed to explain how this all came about anyway. But he called himself going to chew me out in front of the whole A&R department, and he was not about to front me off and belittle me in front of my colleagues. He said, "What are you doing passing yourself off as the president? I'm the president of this company!" First, I tried to explain to him that I didn't know Walter Winchell, nor did I talk to him, and I certainly hadn't passed myself off as the president of anything. He didn't believe anything I had to say. There was only so much that I could take of him insulting me, and finally it got to the point where he pissed me off, and I told him to fuck off! And that was the end of that.

I stormed out of his office, and Bob Morgan, who was head of the A&R department, came after me pleading for me to come on back in. Bob attempted to reason with me by saying, "He's just mad because they've got your name in there and not his." So I returned to Chicago knowing that my days at CBS were numbered.

It wasn't six months later that they showed up in Chicago. My engineer Jim Felix called me at home and informed me that Len Levy and Bob Morgan were over there, asking him all kinds of questions about if I take tapes home, and whether all the masters are where they're supposed to be. I told Jim, "Yeah, why wouldn't they be?" Just as I had anticipated, the shit had started.

Then my secretary Adrienne called me and said, "They're in your office, and they're going through your file cabinets and asking me all kinds of questions." That ticked me off. I said, "I'm on my way down there right now." I drove down there, and found them both sitting in my office as if they had just arrived. We went into a conference room, where they asked me for my resignation, saying that they were going to go in a different direction. They asked me to give them my credit card, which was an American Express, and what they called an Air Travel card. I had to turn that in. They gave me a check for $20,000 for severance pay. Adrienne was in tears because she felt so bad for me. So I just got my jacket and left. It was the first time I had ever been fired. And I must admit, it hurt my pride – it hurt really bad. But as the saying goes, behind every dark cloud, there is a silver lining.

I called home and told Mabel that I had just gotten fired. Even though it was technically a resignation, I took it as a termination. That's when she told me, "You know what, Carl? I've got a calendar here. I'm going to mark this day down, and a year from today we'll look at it and we'll see where you are and where they are. Honey, this turn of events is going to be the best thing that ever happened to you. You wait and see." My wife's words of encouragement were like rays of sunlight breaking through thick clouds of despair, giving the light of hope for the brighter days that lie ahead.

A year had come and gone, and sure enough, I was hot as a firecracker, even though I don't know whatever happened to Len Levy. Just like my wife said, it was the best thing that had ever happened to me. When I left Columbia, I had to leave Major Lance and Walter Jackson behind. They were signed to the label, and other producers took over. But I stayed in touch with them, and eventually I'd record both again.

I still had plenty of irons in the fire. In 1963, I had gone into partnership with Irv Nahan, a roly-poly little Jewish guy in Philadelphia who headed Jalynne Corporation, a music publishing outfit. The firm was named after famed Philadelphia deejay Georgie Woods' two daughters, Jane and Lynne. Irv had briefly co-owned a record label also named Jalynne during the early '60s, releasing singles by Joe Tex and Donnie Elbert, as well as another more prolific Philly label, Red Top Records.

Irv and I began our association as a result of Jerry Butler's writers encouraging me to get into the publishing end of the business as a way to get my songs out there. Irv called one day and asked me to come to Philly. After arriving there, we met and he discussed a partnership with me. He offered me a piece of the company if I would agree to publish my writers through Jalynne. I thought that was an excellent idea and a great opportunity, so I agreed. The first song I published through Jalynne was Mary Wells' "Dear Lover." Since I was no longer employed by CBS, I was able to take full credit for producing Mary's recording.

I also bought into Irv's booking agency, Queens Artists. It was headquartered at 1650 Broadway in Manhattan, at the epicenter of New York's record business district. I had ten percent of the booking agency; my other partners at Queens included Jerry Butler and Curtis Mayfield. I think Ruth Bowen, Dinah Washington's former manager, still had a percentage too. That's why they named it Queens Artists, because Dinah Washington was the queen. We took it over after Dinah's death.

Irv had a very nice three-story townhouse in Philadelphia. I stayed there on occasion. His home was spacious and had offices in the basement and on the first floor, and living quarters upstairs. There was a delicatessen right on the corner where Irv went all the time to get Philly cheese steak sandwiches. He put my name on the mortgage as the owner, and he and I owned the publishing company together. Irv taught me all the ends and outs of the publishing business and showed me how much revenue could be made from publishing royalties.

One time I took Otis Leavill to Philadelphia to meet Irv. Otis had written several songs that he signed to Jalynne Corporation. Otis didn't realize that he had some significant royalties coming from this. We were at Irv's office, and I told Otis to go downstairs to see the secretary, because he had some writer's royalties coming. He went downstairs, she got out the books and added up all the stuff that we were doing, and wrote the check out for three-thousand dollars. He took the check without really looking at it, and stuffed it into his jacket pocket. He assumed that it was only a few bucks, thirty or so dollars.

When he got home, he went to the drug store where he worked, and asked his boss to cash this little check for him. The boss said ok and took the check from him. Then all of a sudden, his eyes almost jumped out of his head, and he said, "Man, I can't cash this check!" Otis frowned up and asked, "Why not?" "It's for three thousand dollars, that's why. I don't make that much the whole week!" Otis took the check and looked at it, and couldn't believe his eyes. So Otis called me all excited. "Carl, this check I got is for three-thousand dollars!" I chuckled and said, "Yeah I know!" I'm sure it was the first time he had ever received a check so large.

In 1965, Irv helped me set up several deals for me to produce artists for Philadelphia's Cameo-Parkway Records. Chubby Checker, Dee Dee Sharp, and the Orlons had been three of the label's top acts at one time. Chubby's "Twist" and Dee Dee Sharp's "Mashed Potatoes" were big national hits earlier in the decade, but by now they had cooled off dramatically. However, on occasion I would run into Chubby at the Uptown Theater, and he was always in my face about getting a shot at having another hit record, so I finally relented and decided to go ahead and produce him.

We recorded, "You Just Don't Know (What You Do To Me)," which wasn't a hit for Chubby back then, but now it's worshiped by England's Northern Soul constituency. We also cut Dee Dee's "Standing In The Need Of Love" and "It's A Funny Situation." We did what we could to give the finished product the best chance possible. We solicited the arranging skills of Riley Hampton and the songs were written by Barrett Strong. These were nice sides for Dee Dee, but we couldn't get them on the charts.

While working in the music business, I have found myself in some very interesting situations, some congenial, some compromising. Not everyone who is associated with this business is an artist or one of the creative types who bring their own unique drama to the scene. However, this business can be filled with thrills. It can also be wrought with peril, and in extreme cases, even danger. In this case, for me it was the latter. While working with Irv, I used to travel back and forth from Philadelphia to New York often. One particular day, I was walking down Broadway in Manhattan with my friend Larry Maxwell, promotions man and owner of the Maxx label. It was a typical day in the Big Apple: crowded streets, throngs of pedestrians, and noisy traffic. Amidst all the chaotic hustle and bustle, we heard the sound of desperate footsteps running behind us. Somewhat startled, we suddenly turned around, and there was one of Irv's promotions guys named Joey, who had almost broken his neck to catch up with us. Frantic and winded, he uttered these chilling words:

"Carl, there is a contract out on Irv."

"What! Who the hell told you that?" I replied.

"I heard it for myself. It's true, they're going to kill him" he insisted.

He then went on to explain that while he was having dinner at a restaurant, he went to use the restroom. After entering, he walked in on two wise-guys talking about Irv. "They didn't know who I was, so I pretended not to hear anything while they talked. They were saying how they were going to put a couple of slugs in that little kike's brain."

Damn! How in the world did Irv get himself in this mess? I didn't know what to do, or who to call. I asked Larry, "You know anybody who's connected to the mob?" Larry replied, "I know one guy named Tommy, who produces some Vegas acts. I think he's connected." So he made the call to this Tommy person, and sure enough, he was a wise-guy. When Larry told them the gist of why we needed this meeting, he agreed to meet. They had us come to this small Italian restaurant over in Queens. Once we arrived, Larry spotted Tommy and went over to greet them, while I stayed back. Larry briefly met with Tommy and this other Italian guy whose name I never knew. Both these men could have been characters right out of a gangster film. They were burly, with dark hair, sun glasses, the whole bit. They clearly gave the impression of being some guys that you didn't want to screw around with. They told us, "Let's go. We'll ride with you." At that point, I started getting really nervous. I mean, first we had to drive over to Queens, now they're taking us to another undisclosed location. Shit! What have I gotten myself into now?

From there, we drove over to Brooklyn, and by the time we arrived, night had already fallen. We parked by a big old Catholic church. Then they got out and left us in the car. I watched in the rear view mirror as the two of them walked back about a block to a small tavern on the corner.

Meanwhile, we're sitting in the car, for about twenty or so minutes. As each minute ticked by, I was becoming increasingly disparate. Every moment seemed like an hour. I didn't know what to expect. Were we fools for trusting these guys? Was it a setup? I began to complain saying, "Damn

Carl H. Davis, Sr.

Larry, at any minute, we could get ambushed and get cut us to pieces with machine guns and no one would ever know who did it!" The point was well taken. After all this was mob we were dealing with, but neither one of us moved a muscle. We just sat there like two sitting ducks in an a deafening silence that was driving me crazy. Every time a car drove by, I slumped down a little. Every pedestrian that passed by, I checked out.

All of a sudden, the door flung open and scared the hell out of us. It was Tommy. He said, "Yeah, there's a contract out on Irv alright. Are you sure that Irv wasn't messing around with some made man's wife or something?" I said, "No, not that I know of. Besides, Irv likes black girls. He wasn't messing around with nobody like that." He said, "Well, something's wrong, because they've got a contract. But here's the deal. We got two issues to deal with. In order to get this contract canceled, you're going to have to cut a deal. And second, we got to reach out into the street and find the guys that actually had this contract, to call these guys in. So my advice to you in the meantime is get Irv out of town until we clean all this up."

During this time, Mary Wells and I were an item and I was staying at her place. I asked her if Irv could stay at her place while I made arrangements to get him out of town. Then I sent Larry out to La Guardia Airport to get a ticket for Irv to fly to Chicago. I was going to let Irv stay at my apartment on the 57th floor at Marina Towers. So I arranged for Otis Leavill and Gene Chandler to pick Irv up at Midway Airport.

Soon after Irv had gotten settled into my apartment in Chicago, back in New York, we had to meet with the mafia guys again. They informed us that they were able to get in touch with the hit-men assigned to carry out the contract on Irv and called them off. They said, "Okay, you've got to send for Irv." So we called Irv and he flew back to New York.

We met him, and we went back out to this tavern in Brooklyn. When we entered this place, it was the typical little watering hole. We walked through the tavern, and entered this back room. It was a dark, dingy, cigarette smoke filled atmosphere. The only distinguishable thing in this dimly lit room was this round table that was situated in the middle of the floor. There was one covered light hanging down from the ceiling illuminating the table and chairs below it. There was an old guy sitting there, and Tommy was there, and me, Larry, and Irv.

Out of the corner of my eyes, I caught the movement of a shadowy

The Man Behind the Music

figure, leaning back against the wall with his arms folded. In the opposite corner was another ominous figure standing there as well. As they stood there in silence observing the meeting, I could almost feel their menacing stare burning holes in the back of my head. I figured that these sinister characters must have been enforcers, there for security. Once the meeting started, Tommy, who was a really tough guy himself, started hollering at these guys.

He said, "You dumb sons-of-bitches! You had all this time to do what you were supposed to do, and you didn't do nothing. Why?" Quickly, they jumped up to their own defense, saying that it wasn't their fault. They said, "Well, one time we had him on a train coming from Philly to New York, but there was too many people in the train, so we didn't want to whack him in front of all those witnesses. And the next time we saw him, he was at the Uptown Theater with Georgie Woods, and they didn't pay us to kill Georgie, so we had to let him slide there, too.

All while these men were mulling over the missed opportunities to kill Irv, Irv was sitting there with sweat running down his face, and scared shitless. Finally, the old guy told them, "All you's just shut the hell up!" Then he turned to Irv, who at this point was as white as a ghost, and asked him if he managed the Drifters; one of the biggest R&B vocal groups in the country. Irv said he did. The old guy said, "Well, what's happening is another agency found out that you had opened up your own agency and they were afraid that you were going to take that group from them and put them in yours. So they put a contract out on you." Irv said, "No, I never planned to take them out of there. We already have Gene Chandler and Major Lance, and that's what we were dealing with. Besides, I only have fifty percent of the group anyway."

So then the old guy said, "Well, because of Tommy here, we called off the hit. But the fact remains that we were supposed to be paid ten G's to do this. So somebody's got to pay us the ten grand. Who's the manager of Gene Chandler?"

I replied, "I am."

He said, "Okay, what we want you to do is we want you to sign Gene Chandler up to this label called Brunswick Records in New York. We're gonna sign him for a fifty thousand dollar advance. And twenty percent of fifty grand is ten grand. So when you get the check, you go over to this bank and you cash it. The Chandler guy keeps forty thousand, and that'll leave you the ten to pay us." Which is exactly what we did. And that's how we took the hit off of Irv, but I never did get my ten grand back. This turned out to be my unwitting induction into Brunswick Records.

I only stayed affiliated with Queens Booking for a few years after this. The company did well for awhile, but then it was wrecked because the Mob completely infiltrated. Since these wise-guys were able to save Irv from getting whacked, they felt like he owed them ongoing favors. They just simply took over, and thought they had the right to hang out up there. Whenever you went to Queens Booking and would go into the conference room, there would be a bunch of hoods sitting around smoking cigars, drinking and talking a bunch of crap about how they were going to shake down this one, or how they were going to extort that one. People started avoiding this place like the plague, because there was such a negative vibe up there.

After Constellation Records folded, Ewart Abner was trying to make some money, so he had worked out a deal with Leonard Chess for Gene Chandler. Abner had committed to recording fresh Chandler sides for Chess. So when my new friend Tommy called Abner and told him, "Give Gene Chandler a release because we're going to sign him to Brunswick," Abner gave him that release. However, he was still committed to Leonard Chess for those particular sides. Then Abner called me and asked me to go with him to Leonard's office to discuss this thing.

Leonard and Phil Chess still ran the top R&B record company in town. Their artist roster ranged from longtime blues mainstays Muddy Waters, Howlin' Wolf, and Bo Diddley, to soul hitmakers Etta James, Fontella Bass, and Little Milton, and jazz pianist Ramsey Lewis. In addition, the Chess brothers owned WVON-AM, Chicago's top soul radio station. Leonard really felt that he had mastered the black sound. So Leonard fell in with the most gritty of musical movements and recorded some of the more progressive and successful blues artists of the time. He felt that he was on the same level and could identify with black artists when it came to R&B product. He had a lot of blacks working for him in all kinds of positions, and many of the blacks probably accepted him as being one of the brothers. He would frequently be heard using idiomatic expressions and vernacular typically associated with black people, and he tried his best to even come across as a soul-brother himself.

During the meeting between Abner, myself, Leonard and Phil about

The Man Behind the Music

Gene's recording future, Leonard crossed the line and called me a nigger. Oh, hell no! All that "I'm a cool soul-brother, I'm really one of you" patronizing crap wasn't about to wash with me. As far as I was concerned, white boys don't call black people niggers unless they're ready to fight. So I became pissed and told Leonard, "You don't know me like that, and you don't address me in that manner!" Leonard was shocked at my tone, and his brother Phil tried to smooth things over by saying, "Carl, you know how Leonard is and how he thinks he's one of you guys." Well, I took exception to that notion, too. I told Phil he wasn't one of us! And I thought that it was time that Leonard stopped disrespecting blacks anyway. Besides, I always felt he was patronizing, and in a sly way getting to use derogatory terms towards blacks (supposedly in a befriending way). I have always been the type of person who gives respect, so I expect to be respected in return.

The net effect of all of this was that Gene Chandler was now signed to two competing record companies at the same time, and I, too, was caught in the middle because I would be producing his records for both companies. We had to find a way to coexist. So I called Nat Tarnopol, the boss at Brunswick. I said, "Listen, it doesn't make sense for us to put out a record and then Chess puts out a record at the same time. We're bumping heads. It's not doing anything for Gene." So Nat agreed that when Leonard released a record by Gene, we would not release one. And when we released one, Leonard would not release one. It worked out pretty well. We didn't have any problems with it after that.

Gene scored several hits for Brunswick. "The Girl Don't Care" and "There Goes The Lover" in 1968 were the cover to James Brown's "There Was A Time." We also did two duets with my secretary, Barbara Acklin. They were interspersed with hits for Leonard and Phil's Checker subsidiary, timed so they wouldn't directly compete with Gene's Brunswick output. I think our agreement probably served everybody well. Incidentally, those Chandler singles on Checker were the only records I ever produced directly for Leonard Chess.

After a lot of years and a lot of hits, I parted company with Gene Chandler near the end of the decade. I had to ask him to leave my office because he disrespected Otis Leavill. I think Gene said something derogatory to Otis that ticked him off. Otis was from the streets and used to belong to a gang. He wouldn't take nothing from nobody. So they got into this heated argument, and Gene tried to make Otis look bad. I knew there was no good ending to this situation, so I intervened.

I said, "You know what? If you don't like what's going on up here and you don't want to be a part of what we're trying to do, you pack up, Gene Chandler, and you get out of here. Because you're not going to make the whole barrel rotten. If you think you're so great, you can do it on your own!" When he left, he took my receptionist. She left and went to work for him, and he talked my bassist Bernard Reed into leaving, and a couple of other people. He opened his own office right down the street at 13th and Michigan and had some success with a duo out of St. Louis called Mel & Tim. He produced their 1969 hit "Backfield In Motion" for the Bamboo label. He signed himself as an artist with Mercury and had his own hit the next year with "Groovy Situation."

Well, the grass wasn't greener on the other side after all. It was only about three weeks later that every one of them called wanting to come back. Initially, I told them, "No, I don't want none of y'all back." But then Eugene Record came to me and said, "Man, we need Beanie," which is Bernard. So I said, "Okay, but you've got to explain to Bernard that he's either for me, or against me. If he's not gonna be a part of what we're trying to get done, he's a part of the problem, and I don't need that." So we took Bernard back. But I didn't take the receptionist back. She was Sonny Sanders' girlfriend at the time. I just couldn't allow it, because Gene was very negative and he was always challenging me. Gene Chandler had an attitude and an ego problem, and was always challenging everybody back then.

Eventually, we'd reunite to cut more hits, and today he's one of my best friends. We see each other quite a bit now. But back then, we were like oil and water – we just didn't mix very well.

Chapter 6

As I stated earlier, in the beginning, being let go from CBS was a very difficult transition for me. However, it was my wife who really encouraged me to charge forward despite this seemingly overwhelming setback. Her warm words of encouragement set the stage for me to launch out into the deep. Therefore, I didn't waste any time and I opened an office over a restaurant at Roosevelt and Wabash Avenue. It was located smack dab at the northern end of Record Row. It was a bare office space that needed to be completely built out. Otis Leavill and I went to a hardware store and bought all the wood, drywall, paint and other building material that would be needed to complete the construction of our office. Otis had become indispensable to me in the day-to-day operation of the company. With the help of some members of the Artistics, Otis and I started transforming the place into the new Chicago headquarters of Jalynne Corporation.

    Everybody wanted to pitch in. Otis was more knowledgeable concerning construction than I was, and he drew up the plans and framed out the offices and the reception area. We also built a rehearsal studio where we could make demos. After we erected the walls and got them painted, we laid some beautiful red and black tile throughout the office. However, in the reception area, we installed a different color tile. In my office we laid carpeting. We did every bit of the remodeling ourselves, except for the existing four offices that looked out onto Wabash Avenue. When we got finished, our headquarters office was something to be proud of. I received a great feeling of satisfaction and accomplishment as I looked at the fruit of our hard labor. However, as it turned out, we'd only stay there for a year or so.

In August of 1966, after we signed Gene Chandler to Brunswick, I went to the inaugural Rhythm & Blues Convention at the Waldorf-Astoria Hotel in New York. That's where I first met Nat Tarnopol, the executive vice president of Brunswick Records. Nat was a young Jewish guy who originally came from Detroit. He was about 5'10" and weighed about 165 pounds. At one time, Nat had been an aspiring baseball player who was actually being scouted by the Detroit Tigers and Chicago White Sox. However Nat turned down a baseball career due to the low pay that baseball players made at the time and anti-Semitic sentiments that were prevalent in the league. Nat eventually got a job working for Detroit's Union Tire company, where he had been a truck driver and a tire salesman. In the evenings, Nat used to hang out at the Flame Show Bar in Detroit's Black Bottom section. This is where he met Al Green, who managed several local artists like Johnnie Ray, LaVern Baker, Della Reese, and Jackie Wilson. When Jackie Wilson wanted to leave the group, Billy Ward and the Dominos, it was Nat who convinced Al to sign him. When Green died suddenly in 1957 while in New York to sign Jackie to Brunswick, Nat took over Jackie's management and finalized the deal with Brunswick, at which time, Nat set up shop there in New York.

However, by the time I met Nat, Brunswick had fallen on hard times. That's when Nat asked me to produce one of his artists. I asked him who it was. Nat responded with a smile, "Jackie Wilson." Wow, I thought. Jackie is someone I had idolized for years. I certainly remember when I used to see him backstage at the Regal years ago when I worked for Al Benson. It was amazing. After all those smashes he made during the late '50s and early '60s for Brunswick, Jackie had fallen into a deep slump on the charts and needed to have his career jump started, and I was the one to do it. It was also evident that not only did Jackie really need another hit, he needed a complete makeover to the more contemporary sound that was happening at the time.

I told Nat, "I'll have to meet with him first. It's important that I have a feel for a person before I agree to work with them." So he arranged for me to meet with Jackie in New York. Jackie lived in an apartment in this big high-rise building. I went up there, and I met his lovely wife and his little son. One thing that I liked about his apartment was he had a big pool table. I used to kid around with Jackie and ask him, "How in the hell did you get this pool table in this house?" We shot some pool and talked, and that's where we began to forge a long friendship between us.

Now that I had met with Jackie, I had him come to Chicago and meet my staff, so that we could all feel good about what we were doing. As I suspected, Jackie hit it off with everybody. He came out to my house and met my wife and kids. He brought his kid out. We all hit it off really great.

Soon after that, we went to work. My receptionist, Barbara Acklin, wrote the first single we did on him, "Whispers (Gettin' Louder)," with David Scott, a member of the Five Du-Tones. My thanks to Otis Leavill because he was the one who had brought Barbara into the company. When we built our office at Roosevelt and Wabash, Barbara's desk was stationed in the reception area, and my office was behind that. Jackie was there at our office because we were going over some different songs. Since Barbara was the receptionist, she would always see him and that was enough to inspire her to try to get him to sing one of her songs. One day Barbara came into my office and said that she had this one song, and she wanted to play it for Jackie. I told her, "Go ahead on in there!" So she went in there and started singing the song, and then Jackie came and told me, "Man, I want to do that! I want to do Barbara's tune." I've got to give it to her, she's the one that got Jackie to do "Whispers."

After we finished cutting Jackie's first session, I knew we had a big hit on our hands. So I took the song out to New York. They had called Berle Adams and all the big shots from Decca, Brunswick's parent company, down to this big conference room. There we were, sitting around the table, so I put the record on and played it. Everybody loved it. The song instantly rejuvenated Jackie's career, soaring to number five on the R&B charts and number eleven on the pop charts in late 1966. That October, Nat named me Brunswick's A&R director.

Working with Jackie was just a pleasure. With some artists, working with them was like pulling teeth. But whatever you asked Jackie to do, he would do it. Even if there were some tunes that he may not have preferred, like those bubblegum songs, Jackie would still put his all into it. He was a true professional. He could do opera. He could do anything. So you tried to find some songs that were the right fit for him, while also having the commercial appeal necessary to promote strong record sales and revenues.

It was such a joy to sit with him and play different songs for him. I can still picture Jackie with his little bounce. He had that little bounce about everything he did, so we used to try to come up with something that had that little bouncy thing to it. I loved working with Jackie. At times, you would think he wasn't paying attention until you turned on the track. And what came out of his mouth was superb.

Jackie's voice had a nice range to it. He had one note that he could effortlessly take up a couple of octaves – it was sky-high. Every now and then when he was riffing, he would hit that note. Whenever he'd be taping, he'd be looking right at me in the engineer's booth. I'd just point up and he'd give me what I ended up calling the bird note (because it was so darned high). Jackie was the type of musician who could give you whatever you needed on cue. If you wanted something, you just let him know that you wanted it. Where other people might take three and four takes on it, he'd do it on the first take. And when you heard him do it, you'd say, "That's it! That's a wrap. We don't need to do another take, because that's it!"

Jackie's next hit was in the spring of '67, "I Don't Want To Lose You." I'm down as co-writer with Karl Tarleton. A lot of times these songwriters would come in and play a song for me and say, "By the way, you own fifty percent of that," just to get me to do it. And of course, I would take it. If they were willing to give it to me, I'd take it. Some tunes I did help write, but most of the songs with my name down as co-writer were just given to me. Sharing the writer credits and the royalties was not that uncommon back in those days.

However, by far the biggest seller that I ever produced on Jackie was "(Your Love Keeps Lifting Me) Higher and Higher," a number one R&B smash in the autumn of 1967 that blasted up to number six on the pop charts. Instead of using my house band, I brought in Motown's Funk Brothers, including bassist James Jamerson, to lay down the rhythm track. We used the Funk Brothers on a lot of songs with Jackie, who was a Motor City native himself. I would pay them double scale in cash, so they loved to engage in a little moonlighting for me. In addition to the Funk Brothers, Motown's in-house female vocal group, the Andantes, came along to provide their gospel-tinged background blend on "Higher And Higher." I think the only time we used the Andantes was with Jackie Wilson.

When I finished the rhythm track for "Higher And Higher," I brought it to New York so Jackie could cut his vocals. When we went into the studio and he started singing it, it was completely different from what I thought it should sound like. I told him, "No, no, no, no. I don't like that!"

He said, "What's up, Boobie?" I don't know where he got the name "Boobie" from. I think he gave that name to people he liked. So he told me, "Well, come out here and sing it how you want it sung." So I came out and sang the melody for him. He said, "Oh, that's what you want?" He went back in there, and knocked it out of the park in one take.

One of my staff writers named Gary Jackson was the one who brought me "Higher And Higher." However, he told me that one other guy named Carl Smith had written it with him. When we went to the studio, I put it under Brunswick's publishing company. And no one else claimed any rights to it. However, once it became a major hit, writers started coming out of the woodwork. Billy Davis at Chess said he was in on writing it, and Chess staffer Raynard Miner said he was in on writing it, too.

If that weren't enough, it turned out that my old friends, the Dells, had recorded "Higher And Higher" for Chess right before Jackie did it. This was a big mess. I was so glad I didn't put it in my publishing company. I just told them, "Hey, y'all straighten it out." Gary had led us to believe that it was just him and Smith who had written it. But they ended up splitting it all up, with the final credits going to Jackson, Smith, and Miner. Fortunately, Nat was able to get it all straightened out.

Despite that hassle, Gary Jackson made good and brought me another tune for Jackie, "The Who Who Song." It was right down Jackie's alley and I loved it. However, it was the B-side of that single, "Since You Showed Me How To Be Happy," written by Gary, Gerald Sims and another staff writer, Floyd Smith, that was Wilson's next sizable hit at year's end. Jackie was on a hot streak. We released more solid sellers on Jackie after that, one written by Van McCoy titled "I Get The Sweetest Feeling" in 1968 and "This Love Is Real," written by Jack Daniels and Johnny Moore, at the end of '70.

When you are famous and making money, you tend to attract some very shady characters. The same is true for Jackie Wilson. I've heard stories about Jackie being hung out of a window at a high-rise in Manhattan, over some financial misdealings. Apparently, he owed somebody some money, or there was a dispute over signing a contract or whatever. I personally do not have any direct knowledge of that incident. However, decades later when a member of the Dells was doing a television interview about the film "The Five Heartbeats" (released in 1991 about a fictitious group, but based on some actual experiences of the Dells), he said that the scene where a singer was dangled out of a window was actually about Jackie Wilson.

It's true that Jackie did have some rough characters intimately involved in his career. He personally told me that some hoods came and got him and took him somewhere, where they forced him downstairs to some dingy basement, gagged him and tied him to a chair in a dark musty room. Jackie said the room was full of rats because he could hear them and they were running all over his feet. They left him down there for about an hour. That too, sounds very scary. After that, whatever it was that they wanted Jackie to do, I'm sure he did it.

Jackie had been Brunswick's flagship artist for a long time when I began producing him. Apart from him and veteran R&B chanteuse LaVern Baker, the label didn't have much going, so I brought several of my artists over. The company's next release after "Whispers" was the Artistics' long-awaited breakthrough hit. Written by their own Jesse Bolian, Larry Johnson, and Marvin Smith, "I'm Gonna Miss You" finally brought them much-deserved stardom in late '66. We had listened closely to Motown, and the Four Tops in particular. I think Bernard Reed was the one who came up with its distinctive bass riff. He was really good on that bass. He had it cookin'. Bernard worked a lot with the Artistics as their bandleader, and taught them most of their choreography, so they were really good. And they all looked sharp. We dressed them really nicely, so when we sent them out there, they were ready. I just loved the Artistics. I thought they were the closest thing to Motown that we could get.

Right around that same time, we put out "Time Stopped," a solo Brunswick single by Marvin Smith. It wasn't a big smash, but it did alright. I really wanted him to stay with the Artistics, but it had gotten to the point where they were having some friction, so he left to go on his own. I don't think he ever wanted to be a part of a group. Back in those days, that was what was going on. You had to be a part of a group in order to get out there.

The Man Behind the Music

Then, once you could get established, you could go out as a solo artist. When Marvin left, the Artistics brought in a young guy named Tommy Green as the new lead. He co-wrote their 1967 follow-up hit "Girl I Need You." Marvin had a couple more Brunswick singles of his own, but they didn't do much business.

Billy Butler, now a solo artist, also came over from OKeh, but he didn't have the same luck on the charts as the Artistics. Billy co-wrote his first Brunswick single, "Help Yourself," which came out before the end of 1966. Three more followed that stretched into '68, but we couldn't get any more hits on him. There were a couple of tunes we did on Billy during his Brunswick years that I thought were masterpieces.

As I stated earlier, it was Otis Leavill who brought Barbara Acklin into the company. Though she started out as a receptionist and my secretary, she quickly assumed more duties. One of her responsibilities was to go out and hire background singers. Barbara was no joke. She'd work those singers to death. If they weren't of a certain quality, or they couldn't hack it, she'd fire them. Sometimes we would use a background group, and then we would have Barbara come in a week later and lay down another track on top of theirs, but singing an octave higher. Then we'd mix it all together. It worked well because she didn't have to actually sing with all these other groups, but we would use her to lay her tracks later.

I still remember the day that Barbara came to me and said that she was a songwriter. I just said, "Yeah, right." I didn't really pay a lot of attention to her until she wrote Jackie's hit "Whispers." And then she started writing with different artists. She'd write with anybody, because she wanted to get her stuff out. Gene Chandler had the idea to make her his duet partner, and they had two 1968 hits together for Brunswick, "Show Me The Way To Go" and "From The Teacher To The Preacher." He liked doing duets, and he loved doing them with Barbara. He liked the way Barbara sang and so did everybody else. But it was Jackie Wilson who really recognized her great solo potential.

After a while, Jackie started annoying me about producing Barbara. He would always say, "Why don't you do something with Barbara? The girl can sing." I said, "Barbara? Man, Barbara's my secretary. She's my receptionist." He said, "Yeah, but she can sing, too." The truth was, I heard Barbara sing before and I knew she could sing. But I was hesitant because I

Carl H. Davis, Sr.

wasn't really good with women singers, except for the Opals, so I basically didn't want to be bothered with producing her. But Jackie was relentless, and eventually he started saying, "If you don't want to do it, then let me produce her for Brunswick."

By that time, the Chi-Lites' Eugene Record and Barbara had started dating. Before that, she'd been seeing Quinton Joseph, our studio drummer. So Eugene ended up writing several songs for her. After Jackie kept bugging us, I told Eugene, "Please find something for Barbara to do so we can take her in the studio." I loved Jackie, but he was really getting on my nerves concerning Barbara. But looking back on it, I'm glad he stayed on me about it, even though Jackie didn't end up producing her.

Barbara's first two solo singles, neither of which Eugene wrote, slipped through the cracks. But Barbara really broke through during the summer of 1968 when Eugene got together with Gerald Sims and Sonny Sanders to write her "Love Makes A Woman." Eugene produced it, and my brother Clifford played the sax solo.

After we got "Love Makes A Woman" completed, I went to New York to visit Brunswick, which was still a part of the Decca Records hierarchy. I went up there and gave "Love Makes A Woman" to Nat, and he played it. I could tell he really didn't know what to think about it, but he was wise enough not to berate it since he knew that I was behind it. So instead giving his opinion, he asked me the obvious. Nat asked, "So what do you think, Carl?" I said, "I think it's a smash!" Since I said it was a smash, Nat, who had complete confidence in me, said, "If Carl says it's a smash, then it's a smash!"

After the meeting, I gave it to their promotion man, Joe Medlin, who was a star in his own right at one time. However, when he listened to it, he had the nerve to say,

"Man that ain't nothin'."

With an immediate attitude, I responded, "What did you say?"

He said, "You heard me. I don't hear nothin' in that."

That really pissed me off. I got so mad that I told Nat, "I'll tell you what – you give this damn A&R job to Joe Medlin, since he thinks he knows what's a hit and what's not. I'm not putting up with his crap. I'm outta here!" I stormed out and was heading towards the elevator, when all of a sudden, here comes Joe Medlin, running behind me. "Carl! Carl! Man, they're getting ready to fire me in there."

I said, "I don't like your attitude, Joe. If you're the one who's supposed to promote my product and you have the gumption to tell me you don't like it, that speaks for itself – you ain't gonna promote it!" So I went back in the boardroom and I told them, "All I ask you to do is put my product out, and give it to the jocks. If the jocks tell me that it ain't a record, then fine. I can accept that. But nobody else is going to tell me what is a hit record."

If it had not been for Nat being a part of the team, I probably would have left. Two weeks later, "Love Makes A Woman" was already on its way to number 3 on the R&B charts and number 15 on the pop charts. Needless to say, I got an apology from Joe.

Eugene wrote Barbara's follow-up hit later that year, "Just Ain't No Love," and he and Sonny Sanders were responsible for her '69 hit "Am I The Same Girl." Barbara had more hits for us after that: "After You" in 1969, "I Did It" the next year, 1971's "Lady Lady Lady," and "I Call It Trouble" in '72. Eugene wrote them all in partnership with Barbara. If you look at Eugene's tunes, you'll see Barbara's name on a lot of them as a writer.

One of the main ingredients to fine tuning and perfecting our famous Chicago Sound was to keep the hottest musicians in town on our roster. Some of my studio musicians from the OKeh days had come over to Brunswick with me. My brother Clifford, of course, was still my main tenor saxophonist. John Avant remained on trombone and Murray Watson stayed as one of my trumpeters. Bernard Reed had taken over as bassist, and Quinton Joseph on the drums. Quinton had a very unique drumming style. He was the first and last drummer that I ever saw who played standing up. And amazingly enough, he kept impeccable time. Bernard's brother Danny was one of our guitarists, along with Billy Butler and Danny Leake. Floyd Morris was still my primary keyboardist.

Our in-house musicians always cooked up the hottest grooves in town under the direction of my gifted arrangers, Sonny Sanders, Tom Tom Washington, and Willie Henderson (a baritone saxist brought in by Otis Leavill). Willie would also become one of my top producers. I remember asking Otis to get us a baritone sax player. He knew Willie and brought him in. Back in those days, Motown often featured a baritone player. So everybody else got one, too, because we all tried to copy one another.

Carl H. Davis, Sr.

Willie was very talented in that he could do charts and he could write arrangements. He could take your record home like my brother used to do, and he could write an arrangement for the whole band. So we'd have him do that, and then when we needed a band to go out, he could put a bunch of musicians together who he thought could blend well, and they would just hit the road. Guitarist Gerald Sims was another of our musical directors. We were trying to give everybody some kind of credits on the label, so I often used to list Gerald or Willie as musical director.

Jackie Ross came over from Chess, where she'd had a big hit with "Selfish One," to cut a couple of 1967-68 Brunswick singles. Former Atlantic Records star LaVern Baker, whose "Tweedlee Dee" and "Jim Dandy" were mid-fifties smashes, updated her sound dramatically when Sonny Sanders arranged her '69 Brunswick outing "I'm The One To Do It," penned by Billy Butler and Carl Smith. I never actually produced LaVern. We did some tracks, sent them to New York, and I guess Nat took her in the studio.

Unfortunately, I never had the opportunity to produce my friend Aretha Franklin. The closest I ever got to it was when I co-wrote her older sister Erma's 1969 Brunswick hit "Gotta Fine Me A Lover (24 Hours A Day)" with Eugene Record. Aretha had introduced me to her. I appreciated the fact that Erma didn't try to sound like Aretha, because she had her own unique sound. I decided to take her in the studio.

Fred Hughes was another talented young man who we recorded, but we didn't have as much success with him as I would have liked. By the time he signed with Brunswick, Fred had been on both Vee-Jay, where he had his biggest hit "Ooh Baby, I love You," and Chess Records. I co-produced his 1969 hit "Baby Boy" with Eugene Record and handled his 1970 chart follow-up "I Understand."

One of my biggest instrumental hits turned out to be a smash by default for some instrumental jazz group we ended up naming Young-Holt Unlimited. Bassist Eldee Young and drummer Isaac "Red" Holt had been two-thirds of the Ramsey Lewis Trio since the mid-1950s, playing on Ramsey's 1965 smashes "The 'In' Crowd" and "Hang On Sloopy" for Chess. I'd known Ramsey and the trio for years. Then all of a sudden, for some unknown reason, Ramsey decided he wanted to get some new musicians, so the trio broke up.

One day, Eldee Young and Isaac Holt came by my office, very pissed

The Man Behind the Music

off because Ramsey had let them go. They said that they had gone out and found a piano player named Don Walker who could take Ramsey's place, and they wanted to call themselves the Young-Holt Trio. So I signed them to a contract with Brunswick. We took them in the studio, and we did their instrumental "Wack Wack," which did pretty good at the end of 1966. The trio didn't have any problems getting booked, because all the places that Ramsey ever performed in liked them, too. They made me their manager, so I was making twenty percent off their earnings.

But neither Young nor Holt was anywhere near the studio when we recorded their biggest-selling Brunswick record of all – an instrumental that wasn't even jazz, named "Soulful Strut." This tune started out as a Barbara Acklin rhythm track which featured our house musicians Bernard Reed on bass and Quinton Joseph on drums.

When Barbara sang it and gave us the key for the rhythm track, she must have misjudged what her key was. When it came time for her to sing it, she had a cold and couldn't sing in that key. So we just had the track laying there. She eventually put her voice on it, and it would do pretty well for her in 1969 as "Am I The Same Girl."

One day, I gave my house pianist Floyd Morris the track with Barbara singing on it. It was clear that Barbara was straining to sing. So I directed him to take this track home and write out the chord progressions to exactly what she was singing, because I wanted him to play her vocals on the piano. That's what he did. When I heard the finished product, I liked it, but I didn't know what to do with it. I began pacing back and forth, then I turned and asked Floyd, "You mind if we put your name on it?" He emphatically said, "No, don't put my name on that bubblegum stuff! Oh no. Don't want my name nowhere near it." He was a serious piano player, and didn't want to mess up his reputation, so he wouldn't attach his name to it.

Now I'm searching for someone's name to put on the record so I could release it. During this time, there was a rhythm and blues convention down in Miami. I decided to go down there to look up someone from the Hugh Masekela camp. The South African jazz trumpeter was riding high with a groove similar to "Grazing In The Grass." After meeting with one of the group members, I appealed to him by saying, "I've got a smash song here. I just want to put somebody's name on it and put it out."

The guy said, "Give it to me, and I'll take it back and let Hugh hear it. If he likes it, I'll give you a call." A few days went by and I didn't hear from him, so I called him back. That's when he told me that Hugh didn't like it.

Eldee and Red came over to my house, and I played it for them. They said what everyone else was saying, "Oh no, that's bubblegum stuff." Then Red seemed to have a change of heart and asked to take it home and listen to it. He promised to call me back later. By this time, I was exhausted with trying to find someone's name to put on it. I said, "Okay, but if you don't put your name on it, I'm going to put my name on it and put it out as the Carl Davis Orchestra, because I think it's a smash." Sure enough, he must have called me around 11:30 that night. I was in bed when the phone rang. Red said, "Man, I didn't particularly care for it, but when I played it for my son, he really liked it. So we want you to go ahead and put our name on it."

I called Nat and I said, "Nat, I'm going to put Young-Holt's name on this track." He said, "That's fine, Carl. do whatever you need to." The only problem was, it was clearly not a trio's recording. This was a full orchestra, with strings and everything. So I slightly altered the name and called it "Young-Holt Unlimited." The word "Unlimited" better reflected the idea of a orchestral sound. That was the finishing touch that we needed. When we released this record, it took off like a bat out of hell, just like I knew it would.

Ironically, "Soulful Strut" was a number 3 pop and R&B smash for Young-Holt Unlimited without either Eldee or Red ever playing a single note on it. And it goes without saying that while this record climbed the charts and sold thousands of copies, and while couples stepped to its mellow beat, several people who I had asked to put their name on it were kicking themselves in the end – all but me, Eldee Young and Isaac Holt.

Chapter 7

The summer of 1967 turned out to be another transitional time for not only our company, but for one of the pioneering record companies on Chicago's record row. Just a few years prior to '67, none of us would have imagined that one of the most successful black-owned labels in the country had pressed their last piece of wax. The reign of mighty Vee-Jay had come to an unfortunate end after they filed for bankruptcy and folded. The proverbial axiom suggests that one man's misfortune is another man's gain. This proved to be a truism and an opportunity for me to seize upon.

Vee-Jay was located at 1449 S. Michigan Avenue, only a few blocks from our office at 58 East Roosevelt. When Vee-Jay folded, their building went up for auction. Since the Internal Revenue Service had taken over the property for back taxes, they had a big sale of all the building's contents. Leonard Chess was there when they were auctioning off all the equipment and furniture. It wasn't long before we started bidding against each other. As our counter bidding persisted, we were clearly getting on each other's nerves. At that point, Leonard finally came over to me and said, "Carl, it doesn't make sense for us to bid against one another. You tell me what you want, and I won't bid on it. And I'll tell you what I need, and you don't bid on it." This turned out to be a mutual concession that worked out for both of us. There were some cubicles that had glass panels in them that I wanted, and Leonard wanted stuff like, turntables, speakers, and other equipment. As it turned out, we really didn't want the same things after all. Furthermore, there was more than enough there for both of us anyway.

Besides the equipment and furniture going at auction, there was a lease available on the building as well. I entered into a three year lease and moved our headquarters to this location. This was a big deal for us. Our new headquarters would now be housed in a historical location, where Vee-Jay once reigned. I was so excited. Just to think that I used to be here with all the industry people who hung out at Vee-Jay years ago, and now here I am in my own company occupying the same space as the company that once made us all so proud. During our first leasing term, we only occupied the second floor, but we eventually expanded our operation downstairs as well in the subsequent leases.

After we got all settled in and we changed the sign on the door, that's when all the fun began. We wanted a well oiled production machine. When an artist walked in the front door, they would get everything that they needed to be a finished product. We had choreography taught by Bernard Reed. Clifford was in charge of all the music. We had all the musical arrangements and accompaniments necessary to achieve a polished sound. We could accommodate the traditional R&B grooves, all the way up to a ten or fifteen-piece orchestral arrangement. We even had an Italian tailor out of New York who used to do all our stage outfits. He was an expert who could design stuff for all the artists. Sometimes he would come in from New York and spend a week with us, designing and fitting our acts for their clothes. I'd even have him make suits for my sons when they were kids, but I didn't do that too often because they would outgrow them in a month's time.

With our new headquarters office now completed, the time was right to launch a new label, Dakar Records. The name Dakar was actually taken from my last and first name. Da from Davis and Car from Carl. However, in order to avoid looking too much like Decca, I used a "K" instead of a "C." Besides, it looked better with the "K" in it anyway. After forming Dakar Records, I had the responsibility to maintain weekly salaries for all my employees as well as the studio musicians. Generating enough money to meet our payroll and keeping the house band happy were top priorities for my

The Man Behind the Music

newly formed label.

Throughout all of this, Otis Leavill continued to be my right hand man. He and I were very close. But that didn't mean that we never bumped heads. One day my wife came up to our office to see me, and soon as she walked in, she heard me and Otis cussing and raising hell with each other, all the way down in the lobby. She told me later on that she was thinking, "Whoever is in there yelling back and forth with my husband is going to get their tail fired." That was, until she found out it was me and Otis going at it. She knew I wasn't going to fire him. Otis was about the only one who could argue with me like that and not get fired.

When we first launched Dakar, it was just a local label and publishing company. A singer named Shirley Karol had two of the first five releases. After that, I was happily reunited with my old pal Major Lance, who had been dropped by OKeh. Major's hit streak had wound down considerably when the company shipped him off to record in Nashville with producer Billy Sherrill. However, Major's first Dakar single was a dance number called "Do The Tighten Up," and this time Willie Henderson produced him.

Our label's breakthrough national smash came from a Mississippi-born newcomer to the company, Chicago blues singer Tyrone Fettson. Tyrone had worked as Freddy King's chauffeur and as a road manager for his vocal mentor Harold Burrage, prior to Harold's untimely passing. He'd also made a few singles for the 4 Brothers label as Tyrone The Wonder Boy. That's what he wanted us to call him at Dakar, too. However, I strongly rejected that name. It was too cliché and it did not have the type of commercial appeal that I wanted for my artists. After seeing that the notion of using that name was not going to fly with me, Tyrone came up with a simple spark of genius that quickly solved this problem. He asked if he could use my last name. I agreed. So from that point on, Tyrone Fettson had become Tyrone Davis. I liked it. It had a much better appeal than Tyrone Fettson the Wonder Boy.

When Tyrone came to us, he had this demo of a song burning in his heart that he really wanted us to do. The name of the song was "Can I Change My Mind." When I heard the song, it didn't do anything for me. It was the wrong arrangement for the times, with strings and all that other soft sentimental stuff. I said, "It's a good song, but not the way that it's arranged. It doesn't have any commercial appeal." So he told me that a guy named

Carl H. Davis, Sr.

Wally Roker out of New York had produced it. Fortunately, I knew Wally. So I called him, and we talked about putting another arrangement on it. He said, "Go ahead. I don't have a contract on him. It was just a demo." So I gave it to my arranger Willie Henderson and told him to "funk it up some." And that's exactly what he did. Willie put down another rhythm track and added a snappy horn section. By the time he was finished with it, it came back a greatly improved version of "Can I Change My Mind."

At this point I liked it, but I still didn't see it as the A-side smash. Floyd Smith, one of my house songwriters, had written a song titled "A Woman Needs To Be Loved," which I felt would be the right song for Tyrone's A-side. Everybody else agreed with me. We all thought that would be the hit. So we pressed up some records, and distributed them to our promotions team to promote the A-side, "A Woman Needs To Be Loved." However, all of a sudden, the disc jockeys had turned over the 45 and started playing "Can I Change My Mind," saying the B-side was the smash. But I wasn't willing to concede at that point. I argued, "Oh, no, man. We're going with 'A Woman Needs To Be Loved!'" But it didn't make a difference at that point because they started pushing "Can I Change My Mind," and from there, it just took off. This time I didn't mind being wrong, because I had a hit on my hands.

"Can I Change My Mind" became a smash for Tyrone during the latter months of 1968. However, we did not have the manufacturing resources nor the capital to keep up with the pressing demands. So I flew into New York and met with Atlantic Records' boss Jerry Wexler at his mansion in Westchester. We shot pool and shot the breeze, and we worked out a deal for him to distribute Dakar. With Atlantic's promotional muscle behind it, "Can I Change My Mind" quickly went gold.

Willie remained at the production helm as Tyrone released hit after hit for Dakar: "Is It Something You've Got" in '69, the R&B chart-topper "Turn Back The Hands Of Time," "I'll Be Right Here," and "Let Me Back In." The following year, Tyrone released, "Could I Forget You," "One-Way Ticket," and "You Keep Me Holding On." And the hits just kept coming. 1972's "I Had It All The Time" and "Without You In My Life." "There Is" in '73, and "I Wish It Was Me" in '74. In 1974 when Willie left the company, Otis Leavill and I produced Tyrone's hit "Homewreckers" before Leo Graham took the reins for Tyrone's number one R&B smash "Turning Point" in

The Man Behind the Music

1975. Tyrone was Dakar's flagship artist for as long as we ran the label.

"Can I Change My Mind" wasn't the only Dakar record to benefit from the Atlantic distribution deal, because soon to follow was the sensational Marshall & the Chi-Lites. One day, Otis Leavill came into the office as enthusiastic as I had ever seen him. He was raving about another group he wanted me to hear. Otis said, "Carl, you've got to hear this group called Marshall & the Chi-Lites!" If Otis said they were good, that's all I needed. I said, "Okay, bring them in." The Chi-Lites consisted of Eugene Record (the lead singer and chief writer for the group), Marshall Thompson (who was the sparkplug and out-front man), Robert "Squirrel" Lester (for whom the women swooned), and Creadel "Red" Jones. It was a little unusual that Marshall was out front because the lead singer usually was the one out front. But after seeing the group in action, it made sense. I immediately felt good about them because of Marshall's enthusiasm.

Eugene Record was a nice young man who drove a jitney cab up and down Michigan Avenue to make a living back then. He was a great songwriter, but the only problem with him was that he wasn't sure of himself as a writer and had difficulty distinguishing what was or wasn't a hit song.

One day Eugene came to see me and asked me to hire him as a songwriter so he could stop driving the jitney cab, which would allow him to focus totally on his songwriting craft. I consulted with my partner Nat, and I informed him that I wanted to put a talented young songwriter on the payroll. I suggested that we pay him $150 a week, which was a good salary back then. Nat said, "C.D. (his nickname for me), whatever you want to do, that's fine with me." So I hired Eugene. I got him an office space and he brought his guitar and his amplifier. He'd be back there just plucking away and writing songs. He turned out to be quite a song machine, cranking songs out for a lot of artists. Soon Eugene and Barbara Acklin caught each other's eye and started dating, so he started writing songs for her, too.

Eugene used to come out to my house at night and go down in my basement with his guitar and amp. By this time, I had moved from 87th and Calumet, and I now lived in an affluent community on Chicago's Southside called Pill Hill. I had a huge house right on the corner. We'd go down in the basement, and he'd play different songs for me. He didn't really know what he had. He would play song after song, but he never had an opinion either way about any of them. He kind of put me in mind of Curtis Mayfield, who used to use me as his sounding board to figure out which songs were hit material. I began telling Eugene how impressed I was with his songs, and picked the tunes I thought were hits. It's funny, because he couldn't tell which ones were hits on his own, but he rarely agreed with any of my choices.

The first two singles that we did on the Chi-Lites had actually been released on a different label altogether. Nat asked me to let them make their first record, "Love Me," for Russ Regan's UNI-affiliated Revue Records in 1967. Nat was tight with Russ Regan, and I was, too. I didn't mind doing something for him. Revue also issued the Chi-Lites' follow-up single, "(Um, Um) My Baby Loves Me," as well as two other singles we did on them from one of my songwriters, Lee Charles. However, after the Chi-Lites recorded "The Price Of Love" for Dakar, I insisted that the group drop the name Marshall & the Chi-Lites. Fortunately, Marshall had no problem with that.

About six months after we hired Eugene, he had really found a comfortable pace with his songwriting. That's when he was confronted with the biggest challenge of his life – his young daughter had tragically died. Eugene was understandably very distraught. The day it happened, he came to me in tears, crushed that he had just lost his baby, and heartbroken because he didn't have the money to bury her. I gave him all the money he needed for the funeral. After everything was over, he came and thanked me, and he told me he was going to give me half of everything he wrote. I said, "Gene, you don't have to do that. I would have helped you regardless. Besides, I figured sooner or later you would pay me back when you had it." But Eugene, being the honorable man that he was, felt committed to keep his word. He ended up giving me percentages of some of his songs; a third here, a half there. On Eugene's songs where I share the writing credits, most of them I actually didn't co-write.

We moved the Chi-Lites over to Brunswick after that one Dakar single, and they scored their first Top 10 R&B seller with "Give It Away" in 1969. It was one of Eugene's many hits. In 1971, they had a solid seller in the spring. It was a thought provoking social consciousness song, "(For God's Sake) Give More Power To The People." During the '70s, Black people were really starting to raise their collective voices on many social and economic issues. Black pride and togetherness were at the forefront of many progressive and socially conscious movements throughout the country. Therefore, writer-producers like Curtis Mayfield and groups like the Temptations all found a very receptive audience for these types of songs. When Eugene's song was released, it was a hit because it captured the spirit of the social consciousness of the times. Eugene followed up with another song, "We Are Neighbors," co-written by our house drummer, Quinton Joseph. It also fell into that social awareness groove later that year.

    Those singles were successful in their own right, but when we produced the Chi-Lites' "Have You Seen Her," it was amazing just how huge it was, topping the R&B hit parade and soaring to #3 on the pop charts that autumn. As was typical with Eugene, he wasn't sure about this beautiful ballad's hit potential. His impression was, "It could be a good song for our album." I was much more decisive. I said "No, this might be a good single!" Eugene couldn't see it. He said, "Oh, no, Mr. Davis, this thing is six minutes long!" At that time, radio stations were only playing three-minute songs. Eugene was right about the song's length, but he was wrong about its commercial viability. Everyone loved "Have You Seen Her" anyway.

    In the spring of '72, their next record "Oh Girl" was even bigger, a number one pop and R&B ballad smash. When I heard the song's opening line, I was sold. The hauntingly beautiful opening line, "Oh girl, I'd be in trouble if you left me now," is an R&B classic. Eugene had a lot of faith in me and he learned everything that he could from me. He used to come to every session, and sit there and watch me produce. His attentiveness did pay off, because not only was Eugene writing all the Chi-Lites' hits, he also started producing them as well.

    Ironically, "Oh Girl" became an instant smash hit by way of a very popular prime-time network television show that aired weekly on NBC. The Chi-Lites were to appear on the Flip Wilson variety show, which was the first prime-time television show hosted by an African American entertainer. The night before the show, we stayed at a hotel on Sunset Boulevard, where we got a phone call from the show's producer. He said we had to have a second tune for the show. "A second song," I thought. All of us thought that since "Have You Seen Her" was six minutes long, it would be enough. But on short notice, we found out that this was not the case. It just so happened that we had been working on the rhythm track for "Oh Girl," but that's all we had finished. So we stayed up all night with E. Rodney Jones and Sid McCoy, two disc jockey friends of mine, and worked out the choreography for "Oh Girl." The Chi-Lites performed it on the Flip Wilson show. It was a phenomenal success. Before we returned back to Chicago, there were orders for over five-hundred thousand singles waiting for us.

On the Chi-Lites' 1972 hit "The Coldest Day Of My Life," I'm listed as co-writer with Eugene. That was one of those tunes that we had sat down and talked about, long before we actually recorded it. Originally, he had another concept for the song, but I was hearing a great love song. So that's what we ended up doing. To this day, I still love that song. It's a favorite of mine, not only because I co-wrote it but because at heart, I am a true romantic. I like songs that make you feel good inside. I believe that songs should be experiential. Whenever you hear a song, it should take you to a certain time and place in your own reality. A great song should be like great events in our lives. Whenever you hear a particular song, you should remember what you were doing or who you were with the first time that you heard it. That's a great song, and great songs are what I always endeavored to produce.

My brilliant recording engineer Bruce Swedien enhanced "The Coldest Days Of My Life" with exactly the right sound effects. He knew everything you thought before you thought it. I would tell him, "I hear wind blowing, and water flowing, and thunder!" He'd go out and find those sound effects tapes, and he'd sneak them in there and get them into the records.

The Chi-Lites kept right on scoring big sellers for Brunswick: "A Letter To Myself" and "Stoned Out Of My Mind" in 1973, "Homely Girl," "There Will Never Be Any Peace (Until God Is Seated At The Conference Table)," and "Toby" in '74, always with Eugene their driving creative force.

Dakar had plenty more talented singers on its roster during its early years. My staff writers, Lee Charles and Floyd Smith, had their own singles on the label. So did bluesy soul man Johnny Sayles, a vocal group called the Visitors, and Otis Clay, by then an established R&B star who cut "Baby Jane" with Willie Henderson producing. But the ones who had national success were my old standbys: Major Lance, with his Henderson-produced '69 single "Follow The Leader," and Otis Leavill. His ballad "I Love You," another of Willie's productions, climbed into the R&B Top Ten during the early weeks of 1970. Later that year, Otis had himself another hit, "Love Uprising," with Willie again behind the glass and Tom Tom Washington doing the arranging. Willie also had a 1970 instrumental hit of his own for Brunswick, "Funky Chicken Part 1."

The Man Behind the Music

One of the things that you have to get used to in the music industry is the cross-recruiting that goes on all the time. If you were a hot shot producer or executive, there were people pulling at you to come over to their label. Sometimes this was a good thing, and at other times it boiled down to loyalty and ethics as the basis for declining. Such an incident occurred to me when I went up to Nat's office in New York one day. He informed me that, "Berle Adams and Lew Wasserman want you to head up the rhythm and blues division of Decca. They're going to ask you that, but you tell them no, you're going to stay with me." Sure enough, I was in the restroom, and Berle was in the next stall. He looked over at me and said, "Carl, what do you think about coming to work for us as head of the R&B division?" I told him, "You know what? I appreciate the offer, but Nat Tarnopol brought me in, and he's treated me really good up to now, so I'll stick with Nat." Berle said, "Okay, it was just a thought." I didn't regret it, because anything I asked Nat for, he gave me. I don't care what I asked him for, he would do it.

As the new decade dawned, Brunswick was still operating as a Decca subsidiary. I wasn't totally with Brunswick then. I was just under a production agreement with them, and operating my own company, Dakar, at the same time. But in February of 1970, Nat was so happy with what we'd done with Jackie and the rest of the Brunswick roster that he named me vice president of A&R. In late '71, when my three-year Dakar distribution agreement with Atlantic was up, there would be another deal made.

Nat told me, "I'm having a lot of trouble with Decca. They're saying you've got a label out there (Dakar) that's too close to their label, and they don't want you to have it." So Nat and I made a deal to merge Dakar Records into Brunswick. I merged Julio-Brian Music, my publishing company that I'd named for my two sons Julio and Brian, with BRC Music, which stood for Brunswick Record Corporation. In return, I got 10 percent of Brunswick. In reality, I only received ten percent of Nat's fifty percent, because he only owned fifty percent of the label at that time.

As I look back at it, everything we did back then seemed to turn to gold. I was at the pinnacle of my tenure there at Brunswick. Nat and I were both visionaries. We had a unique vantage point where we were able to see and get ahead of new trends in the music industry. We both had something to prove – me as a record producer and Nat as a label owner. We had something to prove to our naysayers. We had something to prove to our haters,

Carl H. Davis, Sr.

and we certainly had something to prove to Decca Records and MCA. By many, we were called the wonder company, because we came from being a small insignificant company to being a major independent label. My Chicago office became the A&R arm of Brunswick, while Nat took the helm from the New York office. Together, we pooled our resources and talent together, making savvy business deals that caused us to experience exponential growth.

Eventually, Nat got Decca to give him the whole one-hundred percent of Brunswick, which meant I now had 10 percent of the company. Nat didn't get along with Lew Wasserman. And he didn't get along with any of those guys at MCA. For some reason, they didn't like Nat because he didn't fit their mold. Rumor had it that the rift between them was spurred by Nat catching them cooking the books. Fearing that Nat might sue them, they said, "Here, take your label and leave the building!" So Nat opened a new office for Brunswick at 888 7th Avenue in New York.

When we expanded our headquarters at 1449 S. Michigan into the first floor, it opened up a wealth of new possibilities. We built a recording studio on the second floor with Bruce Swedien. On the dials of the 16-track console, he had a picture of his logo, which was a Swedish ship. He was Swedish. He was a master engineer and still is. My brother George, who was heading my publishing department after twenty years in the Air Force, moved his office downstairs to the front part of the first floor, where we also had cubicles for our writers. There was an open space in the middle where we planned to construct a stage, complete with lights, where we could actually train all of our artists on how to perform. In the back, where a warehouse had been, we built a vault to store all of our sixteen and twenty-four track tapes.

Most of the offices remained on the second floor. I had the one located in the front window. Eugene Record was in the office next to me. Right outside of my office, there was a reception area. My secretary was across from there. Then we had more cubicles, with the bookkeeper in one and writers in another. Sonny Sanders' office was up there, and behind that was a lounge with a bar and chairs. Finally, in the rear was the new control room and the studio.

In 1971, right in the middle of all this growth at Brunswick, I expanded my business territory and opened up a nightclub at 87th and Ashland, called the Carl Davis Palace. Even though records were selling and royalties were being generated, it was also important to have revenues for the artists coming in when they were not on the road. So we went out and purchased this nightclub. We found out it was for sale, and we found out that the Italian guy who owned it was connected. Because I was connected too, I went to see him and told him that I thought I could make some money out of this club.

So I bought the club, and then changed the name. It was already called the Palace, so I just added Carl Davis on top of it. I figured, "Okay, when my guys aren't working, they can work in the club that week and make themselves a little money." We'd just take our expenses off the top, and give the artists the door, that way everybody's happy. It worked out well for a while. It was a three-hundred seat nightclub, that generated decent revenues.

I had Gladys Knight & the Pips starring in there. I had Jackie Wilson in there. I had Chuck Jackson, the jazz singer Carmen McRae, and Erma Franklin, Aretha's sister. I also had a lot of my own acts in there, like the Artistics. Most of these artists were also my friends. I had all of them coming and patronizing the establishment when they were not performing. Don Cornelius used to come by there with his girlfriend. When they would ask him to pay his cover charge he would refuse saying, "No, get Carl Davis. I'm a friend of Carl Davis." Somebody would come and holler upstairs, and I'd come down and tell them, "Oh yeah, let him in."

Don and I got to be real close. I was instrumental in helping him with the national pilot show of "Soul Train." While I was working for CBS over on 630 N. McClurg Court, Don got the opportunity to use our location for the pilot show. To help give his new program the star power that it needed, I supplied him with some of his first big acts to appear on his show like, Gene Chandler, Major Lance, the Chi-Lites and others. If Don had eight acts appearing on his show, six of them came from my artist. Not long after that, he was able to take his show out to California with the backing of Johnson Products (the makers of Afro Sheen), where Soul Train became the phenomena that it is today. Soul Train holds the honor of the longest, continuously-running first-run syndicated, music related, program in television history.

As the revenues continued to increase, the Carl Davis Palace attracted a lot of attention – albeit some of it not welcomed. It didn't take

Carl H. Davis, Sr.

long before word reached the Chicago Mob that we were making some serious money. It was obvious. If you placed an order for ten cases of liquor or beer, and then the next week you placed an order for twenty cases, and then thirty cases, they were going to find out. The Mob had a line on everything. They knew exactly what you were doing. But in my case, they couldn't do too much. They confronted me and tried to muscle in on my operation. Whenever the Mob was going to move in on somebody, they would always come to you and say: "I understand you're doing great. Do you want to change your partner?" But I wasn't threatened at all. I'd smile and say, "Naw, that's alright. I've already got one." That was a way of saying I've already got a connected partner – beat it. I'm sure after that, they checked. And needless to say, they didn't come back, so I never had any problems on that end.

Everything was working fine. The Carl Davis Palace was the place to be seen on the Southside, or just to come and hang out. I had a little apartment upstairs which doubled as dressing rooms if you had some artists up there. Some of my kids would even have little shows in the place. We'd take all the liquor off the bar, and they would do their little shows in there. I enjoyed it, but I wasn't really there most of the time. I just had the place, and I had some people who worked for me at the music company managing the club. Unfortunately, that only created an opportunity for some of them to start ripping me off. I found out that the guy I had in charge was watering down the liquor. Others were taking money from the cash register or just simply putting money in their pockets. Since there was no way for me to adequately monitor club activities and it just became a headache, I sold the place and got out of the nightclub business after about three short years.

Chapter 8

There comes a time in everyone's life where we must put everything into perspective. Only so much emphasis should be placed on tangible things that people tend to make such a high priority. The material things that we accumulate, the goals that we have accomplished, in the final analysis many of these are non-essentials. But when it really comes down to it, we must all come to grips with what's really important. Certainly, material things have their place but, they tend to come and go. The glitz and glamour eventually fades and when that happens, often what you're left with is stark reality. This is when you find out who you really are and what you're really made of. The biggest mistake that anyone can make is to think that we are impervious to hardship or that we are exempt from personal tragedy and loss.

My lovely wife Mabel, as feminine as she was, was known around her neighborhood as a tomboy when she was growing up. She used to love to play softball, and she was the back catcher for her team. During one of the games, the batter slung the bat and hit Mabel in the head. The blow to her head weakened one of the blood vessels leading to her brain – although she didn't know it at the time. So there we were decades later, married and with children, and her doctor advised her not to have any more children after

Carl H. Davis, Sr.

Carl Jr. was born. They were afraid that another pregnancy would cause Mabel serious health problems related to the head injury she received as a girl. But she never said anything to me about it because she still wanted to have a little girl. So she got pregnant again anyway, against the advice of her doctor.

Each Christmas, one of my relatives would have family dinner at their homes. We would all come together and enjoy each other's company, celebrating the holiday season. This particular year, Mabel was pregnant but she still wanted to host the family dinner at our house. Mabel told me, "I want to do the Christmas dinner this year." So she went ahead and began planning for the big holiday event. Three days before Christmas, I was down at the studio, when I received an emergency phone call from my next door neighbor, who was Major Lance's mother.

My wife had been taking a shower, when she experienced a sharp pain in her head. She'd always had headaches, and whenever she did, the only thing that would relieve the pain was some medicine she took called Stanback Powder. But this time, the headache was more severe than what she typically experienced. Somehow Mabel was able to get out of the shower, put her bathrobe on, and call Major's mother. The houses were pretty close together there at 87th and Calumet. Back when Major got his hit record, I told him, "You buy this house!" I wanted him to buy the house next to ours for himself, but he bought the house and put his mother in it. Calvin Carter also lived on that same block, and Ewart Abner's sister lived right down the street – like our own neighborhood record row.

Mabel was admitted into the hospital three days before Christmas, so we had to cancel the Christmas dinner at our house. She was in Billings Hospital, which was part of the University of Chicago Hospital complex. I used to go up there every day and see her. However, one day I was at home watching the Chicago Bears football game, and I didn't make it to the hospital. She called me on the phone and she was raising hell, saying, "You get your ass up here now!"

And I said, "Okay, I was just watching the game."

"I don't care about no game! You come up and see me!"

So I jumped in the car and made haste to go see her. When I arrived, she started talking to me about all the bills and stuff. She said, "You know we owe this for this, and this is where I keep this. We've got this over here, and we've got that over there." I said, "What are you telling me all of this for? You take care of that! My job is to make the money. You take care of all the other stuff." But at the time, I failed to pick up on what she was talking about.

All this started on December 23rd. When the new year rolled in, she wasn't getting any better and was still in the hospital. By February of 1968, she was six months pregnant. Then the doctor finally mentioned something about she wasn't supposed to get pregnant. He told me that if she started having labor pains, she could start hemorrhaging inside her head. All this was so overwhelming. I didn't even know what the heck they were talking about!

The doctors told me, "We're okay for right now because the blood clot is up there." The blood clot was keeping the weakened blood vessel from that childhood injury closed. Then one day they called me and told me, "We're going to have to operate because the blood vessel has ruptured and there is serious internal bleeding. Blood is not getting to her brain. We were trying to wait for her to get stronger before we did the operation. But the fact that she is six months pregnant seriously complicates the situation, so we are forced to operate." What this boiled down to is I had to make a very difficult choice. I told them, "I can always have another child. My wife is the priority, so take care of my wife. Do what you have to do to save her." The doctor's response was, "It's not an either/or situation, Mr. Davis. Obviously, we're trying to save your wife. But if we see that we can't save her, then we need your permission to save the child, so that both of them do not expire." Oh my God. How could this be happening? Just a few weeks ago, everything was fine. Now they're talking about my wife may die? Damn it!

What in the world am I going to do? This was so surreal, but the fact remained that one of them was not going to make it out alive.

For awhile, I was adamant. I contested, "If I give you that option, you might let my wife go in order to save the baby." I just couldn't wrap my head around the idea of permitting the doctors to sacrifice my wife. Finally, Mabel's sister Ruby came to me. She said, "Carl, you've got to give them permission to save the child if they can't save Mabel." This was the hardest decision I have ever had to make in my life. And with tears in my eyes I did what had to be done – I relented and gave consent to save my daughter.

A few days after I had given consent, sure enough, they called me at work and told me to come down right away because they were going to perform emergency surgery. I hurried to the hospital and waited in the surgery waiting room. Time seemed to be standing still. Minutes melted into hours. Anxiety and fear only exacerbated my anguish and multiplied my misery. Now there was only one thing in this world that was important to me. All I wanted – more than music, more than wealth or fame – I just wanted my Mabel back. I hoped. I prayed. I waited, hour after each hour. But inevitably, they finally came out and said, "Mr. Davis, we did all that we could." After the doctor said that, I was stunned. I didn't hear anything else after that. It was like I was in the world all by myself, as if nothing else existed. Everything just seemed to fade out like a record coming to its end. I was sucked into a deep dark pit of depression and despair.

    I walked out of the hospital in a daze. I left my car behind and just started walking on that blustery winter day. At the time, we were living at 87th and Calumet, and the hospital was located at 58th and Cottage Grove. I walked for miles on what seemed to me to be the coldest day of my life. But it wasn't the frigid weather that chilled my soul; it was the exposure to the cold reality that Mabel was gone forever. I just couldn't accept that she was gone. My Mabel dead? As the blustery winter wind blew the tears that fell from my eyes, with each step I took in the cold snow, Mabel was on my mind. By the time I got home, apparently an hour or two had lapsed and everybody was looking for me. No one knew where I was. Everybody was worried sick. Their concern was obvious when I finally made it home. This was the hardest thing I've ever gone through in my life.

    As I began thinking back on everything, I realized that Mabel knew she was going to die. When we started having to discuss all the arrangements and business matters, then it hit me, "That's why it took her two months, from December 23 to February 15 – to show me where everything was." Then I found out that she had taken out an additional $20,000 insurance policy on herself that I never knew about. All this stuff that she had set up in advance was her gracious way of preparing for her own departure. It was just like Mabel to always be thinking of others.

    They did save my daughter. But it was still too hard for me to see her because I blamed her for my wife's death – I was in that much pain. My sister-in-law Ruby knew that I was suffering and torn between conflicting emotions. She came to me and said, "They would not have let Mabel die because of the baby. She was going to die Carl, so they had to save the baby." After inducing labor, my daughter was born prematurely at only six months. She was so small that she could fit in the palm of my hand. My daughter Tre'c was born on February 15, 1968 – a very poignant day in my life. Though that's the day my wife's life ended, it was the same day a new life began in my wonderful daughter. Certainly, this is one of the greatest conflicts of my life because through birth came both life and death.

For a while, Ruby and her husband were living around the corner from us in a house they were renting. Even though they were having some marital problems at the time, I offered them the opportunity to move in with me to help me raise Tre'c. There was plenty of room for everyone because we had a four bedroom house. So they decided to take me up on the offer, and moved in with me.

Carl Jr. was five years old at the time all of this was going on. I didn't ever take Carl Jr. to the hospital to see his mother when she was sick because he was too young. However, something of a very odd mystical nature began happening to him. After Mabel died, he started wanting to sleep with me. At first I didn't think anything of it because children often get frightened at night and want to sleep in bed with their parents. So I let him sleep with me for awhile. But one day he said something to me that got my attention in a very unnerving way. He said, "Daddy, can you tell that lady in the green dress to leave me alone?" "What lady son?" I asked. He said, "There's a lady that stands over my bed, and she's trying to talk to me. She always has on that green dress. She's scaring me daddy." That's when it hit me. It's Mabel! Her favorite dress was green!

I wasn't much of a religious man, neither was I the superstitious type. But that night, I got down on my knees, and I prayed and said, "Mabel, the worst thing that could have ever happened is for you to die, because I loved you so much. And now I've got these two kids to raise by myself. But I promise you that I will always take care of them. You don't have to worry about that. When you come to see about Carl Jr., you're scaring him and he is so afraid of you. So promise me that you won't stand over his bed anymore." I guess she must have heard me, because he never told me about seeing her anymore. However, he continued to want to sleep with me for a long time after that.

Mabel's aunt, Rose Gaston, had been with us for some time, taking

Carl H. Davis, Sr.

care of the house and Carl Jr. She originally came from Memphis, and ended up being like a second mom to me. Rose lived with us five days a week and then stayed in another home of mine on the weekends. I'll never find another Rose. She helped me a great deal after Mabel died. She'd clean up and cook, and as the years rolled on, she helped me raise all eight of my kids. I always took good care of her, too. Rose even got along with all of my artists. But that Jackie Wilson was her favorite. Once I had Jackie perform at my nightclub, and Rose jumped up on stage and danced with him. I am eternally grateful for all that Rose did during the most trying time of my life. I could not have made it had she not been covering my back.

In August of 1969, I got married again, this time to Basheba Smith. I called her Beth. Her last married name had been Jackson, but after she divorced, she went back to using her maiden name, which was Smith. She had been a member of that singing group, the Peaches, that Gene Chandler had brought in. In October of 1969, she gave birth to my son Julio, and then we had our beautiful daughter Kelli Beth.

Beth was so gorgeous that she became a professional model. That's her on the cover of Bobby Hebb's *Sunny* album, which came out in 1966, and she was also running on the beach on the front of Ramsey Lewis' *Wade in the Water* LP. She was all over the inside of the gatefold artwork on the Dells' '69 *Always Together* album. I even named a new record label after her: Bashie Records, which was a Dakar subsidiary that was also distributed by Atlantic. During its brief existence in 1969, Bashie released singles by local soul singers Johnny Williams (who would later have some success at Philly International), Johnny Howard, and Wales Wallace. Bashie's logo sported the slogan "The Sound of Chicago."

So Beth and I got married. A guy who owned Chatham Furniture on 87th Street told me about his big, beautiful home in an affluent community called Pill Hill, where a lot of doctors lived (hence the name Pill Hill). At the time, it was mostly white, and only a few blacks lived out there. So I went over and looked at his house. Beth and I loved it. So I bought the house as-is, with everything still in it. He left all the furnishings and everything for the bedroom, the living room, and the kitchen. Beth brought her daughter and I brought Carl Jr., and we moved into this house. Later on, I was able to bring in my daughter Pamela and my son Brian, too. We ended up with a lot of kids at that house.

The Man Behind the Music

Back in the late '60s, there were record conventions held mostly in Miami and Atlanta. Everyone in the rhythm and blues field was in attendance to exhibit their product and to meet deejays and record execs, in hopes of getting a shot at being signed. There was a group at these conventions that called itself the Fair Play Committee, a self-made bunch of guys who threatened to (or actually did) beat up disc jockeys if their records weren't getting airplay. I knew the so-called leaders, but more importantly, they knew me and my connections, so they left me alone and in some cases asked my advice as to who they should jump on. The first convention in Miami doubled as my honeymoon with Beth. I took three or four people with me, and I rented a fishing boat, where I caught a Bonita kingfish and had it mounted as a trophy.

Unfortunately, Beth and I were only married for three years, but we had two beautiful children from that union. Eventually I went to her and asked her if I could raise our two kids with the rest of my children. She agreed. It was important to me to raise all my kids together. I did have to agree to some financial arrangements for Beth, but that was fine with me.

Not too long after the divorce, I caught a bad cold. I went to the doctor, and he gave me a prescription. So I took the prescription to Osco Drugs to get it filled. There was a pharmacist at Osco that I knew named Leo, and he was off that day. So I gave my prescription to this young lady who was on duty. She was looking kind of good, so I mentioned something to her about going out and having a drink.

I said, "Well, I need your phone number."

She said, "You've already got it."

I said, "What do you mean 'I've already got it?'"

"On that bag that says Osco Drug!"

I said, "Okay, that's fine."

I called her, and we set up a date to go somewhere. I told her where I lived, and I told her I had six kids. The next time I got a phone call from her, she said, "You know, I've been thinking about this thing with you and six kids. I don't mean to be rude, but I don't think that we should date or nothing!"

I told her, "Oh, okay. I didn't ask you to marry me. I just said, 'Let's go and have a beer or something.'"

So then I had to go out to California for something. When I got back,

Carl H. Davis, Sr.

I had about fifteen messages from somebody named Dedra Gourdine. I said, "I don't know who the heck that is!" And my secretary came in and said, "Well, she's on the phone right now!"

So I got on the phone and said, "Hello, who's this?"
She said, "Dedra."
I said, "Dedra who?"
She said, "You know, I work at Osco Drug."
I said, "Oh, that Dedra!"
She said, "Well, I've been talking with my mom down in Charleston, South Carolina, and she told me that she thought that it was very rude of me not to go out on a date with you because you had six kids. I was calling you to apologize for that."
I said, "Oh, okay. You still want to go out on a date?"
She said, "I'm not calling you for a date. I'm just calling you to apologize."

Anyway, we went out on a date, and we ended up getting married. I went down to a jewelry store on Michigan and bought a pear-shaped three-karat ring. I got it appraised, and they appraised it at $30,000. I gave it to Dedra one night at home. The next day, she took it straight to a jeweler, to get it appraised for herself. The jeweler told her, "That's a gorgeous ring!"

We got married in 1973, and we've been married ever since. We have two kids, Carleen and Jaime. That makes a total of eight in all, and I raised every one of them.

Chapter 9

Though most of my time and energy has been spent in various aspects of the music industry, sports was my favorite pastime activity. One of the things that I have always enjoyed about Chicago is that there are plenty of professional sports to watch. Chicago is one of the few cities in America that has two major league baseball teams. Since I was a Southsider, I was a diehard White Sox fan. Needless to say, I never did like the Cubs all that much. When I was young, I used to love Bears quarterback Johnny Lujack, and their great running backs like Willie Galimore, Gale Sayers, and Walter Payton. These players, including the great wide receiver Dick Gordon, were among my favorite offensive players. But the Bears were also revered for their defensive game as well. Hall of fame players like Dick Butkus, dubbed the most intimidating defensive middle linebacker in the league, was another one of my all-time Bears favorites. The fact that I was a celebrity in the music business meant that I crossed paths with many of these professional athletes, and I got to know several of them at the height of their playing careers.

Gale lived right down the street from a friend of mine. Somehow or another I met him, and we got to be friends. He was a stock broker during the offseason. Gale had told me about Viacom stock, so I bought four or five thousand dollars' worth from him. I think I kept it until Gale stopped playing, and then I sold it. When I got married to Beth, the wedding reception was at the house in Pill Hill, and Gale was there at the wedding. He stood up with me and took some photos with us.

In my spare time, I was an assistant coach for St. Ailbe Catholic school's eighth grade football team. My first son Brian was a quarterback on the team. My nephews Cameron and Douglas were on the same squad, and Carl Jr. was on the little widget team. I could see that the school's football equipment was either old or worn out, so I bought them new uniforms, helmets, and shoulder pads. Since I knew some pro football players, I asked Gale to write me out some plays. Gale started teaching me about the 2-4-6-8 holes on the right, and the 1-3-5-7 holes on the left. Zero was your center, 1 was your quarterback, 2 was your slot back, 3 was your fullback, and 4 was the running back. He taught me how to combine the two: if you're going through the one-hole with the running back, it was 41.

We taught the kids all these schemes, and also taught them how the numbers called out by the quarterback correlated between positions on the field and game plays. They learned that if you heard 42, you knew the running back was coming through your hole, so you knew how you'd have to block. In order to keep it simple, we drew out the diagrams of the plays. Gale and Dick Gordon wrote it all out for me, and then I copied what they gave me and made a book of the plays so the kids could study them at home. We actually had some pro plays in that book. We had a 5-2 defense, which meant five down and two linebackers. We really had a good team, so it worked out. Gale and Dick never came to any of our practices. They just wrote the plays out for me.

As a result of all the professional consultation, the St. Ailbe's team was very good. We won the championship of the division we were in for the first two years. The other Catholic grammar school priests called our priest and said, "You've got a dead ringer over there, Father, because they look like they're playing professional football!" The priest obviously received considerable pressure from his league opponents, so he came to me and actually suggested that I start losing some games. He said, "Lighten up now, Mr. Davis." But I refused and I told him, "Oh, no, I'm not doing that!" I saw where that was going, so I stopped coaching. I wasn't going to start throwing

The Man Behind the Music

games just because our opponents couldn't handle what we were doing. We weren't cheating. We weren't substituting high school players. They were all the right age. We just had a little professional help from my Bears buddies. Besides, most of the schools that we played also had high school coaches, so they could have provided play consultation if they wanted to.

Brian enrolled at St. Francis High School after he graduated from St. Ailbe. The St. Francis head coach saw that my son was an outstanding quarterback and knew he had potential, so he gave him a scholarship to go there. Brian could hit anything running, he was just that accurate. He had an arm so powerful, he could throw a sixty yard bomb. He made it look so easy. He'd just flip his wrist and that ball would shoot like a bullet. However, when he got to St. Francis, he wasn't assigned to the head coach that scouted him. He was assigned to the coach over the freshmen-sophomore team.

This racist coach saw the superior athletic ability that my son had, but he refused to give Brian a shot at the quarterback's position. He assigned Brian to be a wide receiver, a position Brian was not cut out for nor one he could adjust to. Inevitably, out of frustration, my son lost interest in the team, and went on to drop out of high school all together. Though Brian made his own decision to drop out of school, I still blame that coach for being the reason behind it. Had Brian gotten the chance to play quarterback, he would have eventually gotten a college scholarship. He was just that good.

I stopped coaching football after that until my next door neighbor, who was the principal of Hyde Park High School, asked me to help out at his school. I always believed that God had helped me to acquire the things I had, so I should give back. I went to Hyde Park and bought a 12-man weight and strength station, a seven-man sled, and new uniforms and helmets for the freshman/sophomore team. I coached them to more victories than they'd ever had, with some help from Otis Leavill, Tom Tom Washington, and my son Brian. Carl Jr. played tailback and quarterback on that winning team for a couple of years.

Coaching high school football provided a needed distraction from the hustle and bustle of the music industry. It helped add balance to my life. During the first half of the 1970s, there was room on our roster for some new talent. Our mainstay artists like Jackie Wilson, the Chi-Lites, and Tyrone Davis were all doing fine. But at one point during that time, I heard a group called the Lost Generation, which was a four-man Chicago vocal group consisting of lead singer Lowrell Simon, his brother Fred, Larry Brownlee, and Jesse Dean. My promotions man Gus Redmond brought them in to audition. They used to worry me to death about taking them into the studio, so I finally did. One thing that I noticed right away is that they could write really good songs. Therefore, I decided that we could do some business with those guys. With Eugene Record producing and Tom Tom arranging, they hit the charts running with a song called "The Sly, Slick And The Wicked." It was a #14 R&B seller in 1970. Their encore releases "Wait A Minute," "Someday," and "Talking The Teen Age Language" did well too.

Then Dakar signed Chuck Jackson right after he left Motown. He had a huge baritone voice, and he'd had a lot of success in an uptown soul bag for Wand Records in New York during the early '60s with "I Don't Want To Cry" and "Any Day Now." However, his Motown stint had been commercially uneventful. At some point, I received a phone call from Nat, and he asked me to do something with Chuck. So I agreed, and Chuck came on in and recorded in our in-house studios on South Michigan. I produced his only Dakar single, "The Man And The Woman (The Boy And The Girl)," which Eugene Record wrote. Chuck and I got to be pretty tight. For some reason or other, Chuck and Gene Chandler didn't particularly care for each other. They never actually got into a physical fight, but they did fall out at some point. To me, Chuck was really a nice guy.

We also brought back Johnny Sayles to cut a 1973 album for Dakar. He was a good blues singer. He was a nice guy. He wasn't a pushy kind of guy, he was just around. But I liked him. Several more promising female singers came through our doors. Chicago-born Jean Shy had a couple of early '70s Dakar 45s. She was one of the girls who used to do some backgrounds for us. She was there during that period when we had Karl Tarleton and some of the other guys around there. She was good. Her first release was a version of Nick Ashford and Valerie Simpson's "Keep An Eye" that Willie Henderson produced. My brother Clifford produced her encore, "I'll Belong To You."

Gingi James was into Vegas-style shows, and they wanted me to do a date on her. She had a whole album on Brunswick. I'm credited with producing South African singer Dana Valery, but she mostly just sang over backing tracks that Jackie Wilson and the Chi-Lites had already had success with. Dana sang Curtis Mayfield's swinging "You Baby" on her Brunswick album;

there's another version floating around with my own guide vocal over the same track.

Lyn Roman was a young singer out of California. Under her real name of Linda Griner, she'd made a 1963 single for Motown that was produced by Smokey Robinson. I think Granville White was the one who introduced me to her. She was beautiful, and she wasn't a bad singer either. Brunswick only released one single on Lyn in 1974, "Stop, I Don't Need No Sympathy."

I also got a chance to briefly produce the great Louis Armstrong for Brunswick. He was really a nice guy. He had that distinctive gravelly voice. We got along great. I called Elton John and asked him to send me a song, so he sent me "Sorry Seems to Be The Hardest Word." I sent that to Louis, and we rehearsed it. We went to Las Vegas to cut that song on him. But after we did that song, he died. I don't believe Louis' version was ever released. However, Elton John himself released the song in 1976, and since then, it has been remade by numerous artists.

I never really had a problem with anybody I produced, because I think most of the time my reputation preceded me. People knew that I wasn't taking any crap off anybody. I thought I was as big a star as they were. I liked to do things a certain way, and I wanted you to know your craft. I didn't have any problem with Louis because he knew his craft. I never got to the point where I went into the studio with Sammy Davis, Jr., but I used to go to Vegas to watch him perform because he was managed by Tommy. We'd go down there and get front row seats, then go backstage and hang out with Sammy.

One time I went out there and they put me in touch with the guy who was in charge of all the entertainment at the Thunderbird Hotel. He gave me his suite. He had a living room, a bedroom, and a bath. His clothes were still in the closet. I moved in there, and my friend Tommy would send two of his boys by there. They brought me a big box of wine.

Sammy was real nice. He was exactly the way you would think he would be, the way you saw him with Frank Sinatra and all of them. He was a great guy. He was always joking, kidding around, and he was the fastest draw I ever saw in my life. He would hook on those guns, and he could slap that leather, and those guns would come out real quick. He always had those guns. I don't know if they were real or just cap guns, but in any case, I didn't want him drawing them on me.

Speaking of jazz legends, Lionel Hampton was really close with my partner Nat Tarnopol. Nat wanted me to produce Hamp, but Lionel got sick and he couldn't really do too much right then. I told Nat, "My brother Clifford can play those vibes." So we went into the studio and we did two or three albums that came out under Lionel's name but actually featured my brother playing the vibes on them. I think Brunswick did make an actual album up in New York with Lionel Hampton, but I did most of his albums in Chicago with Clifford on vibes. A lot of times, we used the same tracks that we'd previously had behind the Chi-Lites and Tyrone. "Please Sunrise," for example, is one where we just played the vibes right over Barbara Acklin's old track. You'd just take an old track and have the instrumentalist try to copy the exact melody that the vocalist had sung.

Sydney Joe Qualls was one of the last artists I signed to Dakar (I didn't have anything to do with Bohannon, Dakar's second-biggest artist after Tyrone). Sydney auditioned for Otis first. If you closed your eyes with Sydney, you would hear Al Green. He even came from Al's neck of the woods: Jacknash, Arkansas. This kid sounded just like Al Green. I mean, even the phrasing of his singing. Don't let him sing an Al Green song – you wouldn't be able to tell the difference. During that time, people were a little leery of people who sounded like somebody who was already out there. Now if it had been somebody who died or something, it might have gone over better. Sydney sounded so much like Al Green, it was like he was just trying to copy him.

Nonetheless, we got excited. Sonny and I produced Sydney's 1974 hits "Where The Lillies Grow" and his two-sided follow-up "How Can You Say Goodbye" and "I Enjoy Loving You." But for some reason, he couldn't transcend being an Al Green sound-alike, and that was the biggest problem. We had the same problem with Billy Butler and Jerry Butler. For some reason, people didn't particularly care for somebody who sounded like someone else. I used to preach the evils of that concept when singers would come in to audition and sing Aretha Franklin's "Respect" the same way she sang it.

I used to tell them, "You know, I'm gonna have to pass on you."

"Why?"

"Remember in the future," I would tell them, "never sing every song the same way somebody else sung it. I don't want you to show me how well you can imitate somebody. If you can sing, I want you to take a song that everybody has heard and sing it so that you make it your own. But if you're gonna come in here and sing, "R-E-S-P-E-C-T," all you're doing is making me compare you to Aretha, and that's a comparison you are certain to lose."

Ultimately, that was Sydney Qualls' problem: he just sounded too much like Al Green.

Chapter 10

One of the most popular film genres of our time are movies based on organized crime and Mafia empires. Whether it's classic films like "The Godfather" or more recent productions like the hit cable television series, "The Sopranos," the brutal realities of mob activity are graphically depicted, while their lawless lifestyles are glamorized. Though Mafia film enthusiasts may consider these movies to be sophisticated entertainment, in many cases, they are not just some writer's vivid imagination but are in fact, based upon real persons, places, and things.

Though the allure of the gangster lifestyle is only fantastical to those who experience it in the safe environment of the movie theater, however, there is a real magnetism that captures and envelops those who actually get too close. In the underworld one favor leads to another. One under the table deal digs you in deeper. Associate with a single mob partner, and soon you have many. Owe a dollar, end up paying an arm and a leg for life. These are the unwritten rules – this is how the game is played when you mix with the Mafia.

Before any personal involvement, like most people, I had only known about the Mob through the entertainment media. However, my unwitting introduction to the underworld came when I had to negotiate getting a hit on Irv Nahan called off. That scary initiation, so to speak, immersed me into an entirely new realm of association that I would become quite accustomed to.

Fortunately, I was accepted by some of the Mob bosses in New York due to my relationship with Tommy – a connected man. Tommy has been like a big brother to me. Early on in our relationship, he knew that the person that he should be getting tight with was someone like me, who was making the hit records. He got in touch with me and invited me out to his house. Tommy had a beautiful mansion in Jersey. This was the first time in my life I ever saw a guy with an estate that had its own gas pump. Tommy had major connections in the entertainment industry. He'd been close to Alan Freed during the famous deejay's '50s New York heyday, and he managed several acts. It was Tommy who got the Chi-Lites booked on Flip Wilson's television show, and he got Walter Jackson on Sammy Davis Jr.'s TV variety program.

Tommy wasn't the only one in my immediate business circle with connections. From what I heard, Nat had a friend who was a doctor, and they had gone to a Yankees game together. Nat was a huge Yankees fan, and when they were leaving Yankee Stadium, this elderly guy in the crowd fainted, and had apparently gone into cardiac arrest. Nat's doctor friend acted quickly and successfully revived the man with mouth-to-mouth resuscitation. The guy he revived turned out to be the head of one of New York's Mafia families. I will simply refer to him as "the old man."

The old man was indebted to Nat for saving his life, so he started having people come over to Brunswick to look out for him. But that turned out to be the toehold that they needed to eventually get involved with Brunswick. I believe one of these mob managers also had a management contract on Jackie Wilson. It can be so fascinating and empowering to have these gangster guys around you. These guys had all sorts of privileges and respect that came along with being connected. People feared you when you associated with made individuals, therefore it could be like an addiction to be around these Mob figures.

Everyone back home grew afraid of me because I had been accepted into this new world. However, I was never actually in the Mob, because black people couldn't be in the Mafia. Because of my association with the Mob, they gave me the name of "Chicago Carl." Since I was semi-connected, I was accepted by people who otherwise would have had no business dealings with me. Because of my connections, that all changed and I was respected. I was taught how to say certain things when approached by others in the mob. When cutting deals or solving problems, I would say "You go see who you got to see, and I'll go see who I have to see." Which meant the bosses that we were under had to bless the concerned endeavor. I went to several meetings where I simply passed out my business card to eight or ten people, and was introduced as "our guy in Chicago."

I was asked to meet some people in Rosemont at a restaurant near Chicago's O'Hare Airport. I was told to bring my business cards. When I arrived there, I was told to wait in the lobby. I wasn't certain what the meeting was about, which was typical with these Mafia guys. A lot of times you never knew what was coming. They would just tell you to be at such-and-such a place at such-and-such a time, and you did it. It wasn't long before Tommy came out to the lobby and invited me in. All I did was pass out business cards to well known, made members of the Chicago Mob (who I will reframe from naming). There were at least six to eight of them there. What this did was establish the fact that I belonged to a certain family in New York, but I was operating out of Chicago.

In organized crime, everybody insists on having their orders followed to the letter. If you make a deal to do something, it had better get done. Mobsters tended to have a very short fuse for excuses. Short of the sky falling and the earth being thrown out of orbit, you better do what you were told to do, or else. One hair raising event that I almost got caught up in the middle of all started when my friend E. Rodney Jones and I flew down to Florida one Friday to play golf at the Doral Country Club in Miami. Rodney had left word back at WVON with whomever he left in charge to put this certain record label owner's record on the station's playlist come the following Monday. I'll just call this label owner "Mac," who owned a R&B label out of New York. Rumor was that Mac, a wannabe gangster, had been the driver for one of the big mob bosses. Because of that, he thought he was a wise guy, but he wasn't because there weren't any blacks in the Mob. So Rodney and I went down to Miami and played golf. When we came back to Chicago, I had my chauffeur pick us up in my Rolls Royce, and we dropped Rodney off wherever he was going.

Rodney received a call from Mac, who threatened him, saying:

The Man Behind the Music

"I want you to bring your ass to New York and be ready to get this whippin' I'm gonna put on you!"

Jones responded and said, "What are you talking about?"

Mac said, "Well, my record didn't get played like I told you to do!"

E. Rodney Jones soon found out that someone made an honest mistake which stopped it from making it on the station's playlist when it was supposed to. Jones tried to explain, but Mac wasn't trying to hear it. Instead, Mac insisted, "I want you to come here and bring me my money, and get ready!" So E. Rodney Jones was understandably scared to death. He called me to see what I could do to fix this problem. I called Mac and said, "Mac, Rodney's as good a friend to you as he is to me. How are you gonna send for him to give him some kind of whipping? What are you talking about?"

He said, "Carl, you know what? You remember when that guy who used to work with Curtis Mayfield was getting ready to take one of your songwriters from you, and he asked me to be the buffer between him and you? And I asked him, 'Who you gonna take the writer from?' He said, 'Carl Davis.' I said, 'Oh, no. You can't do that. Carl Davis is too hooked up. You cannot take nothin' from him!' You remember when I did that for you?"

I said, "Yeah, I remember."

He said, "Well, it's the same way here. You can't take nothing from me, because I'm too hooked up! So you stay the hell out of my business with Rodney! I want Rodney to come up here, because he didn't put my record on. You understand?"

I replied, "Yeah I understand, but listen, man – I was there when he left the word to put your record in rotation. Rodney is not trying to play you! Somebody else didn't do what they were supposed to, and I plan on getting to the bottom of it!" After I said that, I hung up the phone.

Needless to say, Rodney was scared to death. So I even called New York, and asked Johnny Roberts, "Can you make sure that nobody bothers him? Mac is saying that he might hurt him." It turned out that Mac was only kidding and just trying to get Rodney up there to hang out with him.

Later on, when I was running my own Chi-Sound label, Tommy and I were sitting around my office on East Huron, when the phone rang. It was Mac on the phone asking if Tommy was there. So I gave the phone to Tommy and Mac informed him that a business associate of ours had a red-hot group on his label, and the group's manager thought our friend was stealing from them. So they were going to send Mac out to California to teach him some manners. They knew that Tommy had something to do with this guy, so they were calling Tommy to alert him about what they were going to do. When Tommy heard this, he asked them to just hold off. He told Mac that he'd be back in New York the next day, and to meet him at a certain place at a certain time so they could get this thing straightened out.

Little did Mac know, by tipping Tommy off that he was going to do harm to one of his people, he really tightened the noose around his own neck. As I stated before, Mac thought he was mob but he wasn't. When he crossed the line to abuse a made man's interest, they made an example out of him. The next thing I heard black gangsters came from 125th Street or wherever it was, and caught Mac and beat him within an inch of his life.

From what I heard after that, the Mafia eventually banished Mac from the United States, sent him to Jamaica or one of those countries, and told him not to come back. But somehow or another, he managed to slip back into Miami because his daughter was getting married. Mac's daughter was friends with my wife's cousin. So her cousin just happened to call my wife Dedra one day, and informed her that she was going down to Miami to attend her girlfriend's wedding. When Dedra found out it was Mac's daughter, she told her "You better talk to my husband first!" I got on the phone and I told her, "You'd better be careful, because from what I understand, Mac is not allowed back in the country and if the wrong people find out that he's back, that's going to create a dangerous situation for anyone around him." Sure enough, Mac called himself sneaking back into the States to attend the wedding in Miami. But before the wedding could happen, they found Mac's dismembered body in a barrel that had washed up on the Ft. Lauderdale shoreline.

Another example of a near miss with the Mob was when Tommy helped me and the Chi-Lites out of a frightening scrape at the pinnacle of their success. The Chi-Lites called me after "Have You Seen Her" started taking off, and they said that they wanted thirty thousand dollars. We'd done a few albums on the group before that, and they were pretty expensive sessions. We were using strings, horns, and rhythm, so their albums were probably costing thirty to forty grand each to record. These were all recoupable expenses, therefore, they actually owed money to Brunswick. Nevertheless, I told them that I'd call Nat to make an appointment to go to Brunswick's

The Man Behind the Music

headquarters in New York to inquire about the matter.

Eugene Record and I went into Nat's office. He was sitting there, along with a henchman that I'll simply call "Johnny." He was like a bodyguard, who doubled as a road manager. I believe it was Johnny's job to go out on the road with Jackie and make sure that his percentage of the take made it back to the bosses in New York.

Once the meeting started, Nat wasted no time in pointing out in a rather intimidating way that they didn't owe the Chi-Lites anything, and he had the sales ledgers with him to prove it. He told Eugene,

"Look at these books. You see where you owe me almost ninety thousand dollars? The Chi-Lites are in the hole, and finally we get a hit album, and now you want thirty thousand dollars, when you already owe me ninety!"

Eugene fired back and said, "Hey, I don't care what you say we owe you. We want our thirty thousand dollars now!"

Before the words could clear Eugene's mouth, Johnny jumped up and grabbed Eugene's nose between his two fingers, twisted it while pulling him toward him, and then knocked the hell out of Eugene. It was so fast, like a grab and punch at the same time.

Then Johnny yells, "You ungrateful cocksucker! This man did all this stuff for you, and he's trying to get a hit!"

The rest of the Chi-Lites were out in the conference room, and they could hear what was going on. This really shook Eugene up something terrible, and he started crying like a baby. However, Johnny wasn't moved by Eugene's tears at all, but said,

"I'm gonna fix this shit now! I'm going to get my fuckin' gun! I'm gonna blow your fuckin' brains out! That's what I'm gonna do!"

So he gets up and he storms out the door. Shit had really hit the fan now. Johnny's sudden outburst even caught Nat by surprise. Nat yelled out, "Johnny, what the hell are you doing?" So he gets up and he follows Johnny out the door. I got up and I locked the door when they went out. I sat back down, and I was holding Eugene. He was crying. I said,

"Gene, I'm not saying that you're not due the money, but you've got to be more tactful than that. You can't just tell the man to go fuck himself, and to just give you the money. These guys are all connected!"

Eugene was scared out of his wits and was whimpering, "The guy's gonna kill me, man!"

I said, "No, he ain't gonna kill you. He can't even get back in here. I locked the damn door, and he can't get back in."

So we're sitting there, and I'm holding him. Finally, I heard somebody knock on the door.

"Who is it?" I asked.

"It's me, Tommy. Open up!"

Thank God it was Tommy, I'd trust him with my life, so I opened the door, and he said, "What the hell's going on?"

I said, "I don't know. That damn Johnny hit Eugene and threatened to kill him."

"What?" Tommy angrily replied.

So then Tommy runs out, and I hear them out there arguing, and I hear him tell Johnny,

"You get the fuck out of here. I don't want to see you no more!"

So Johnny left. And then Tommy and Nat had a little discussion. The end result was, Nat went back into his office and wrote a check for thirty thousand dollars and gave it to me. So I told Eugene, "Hey, I've got what we came here for." Then I went in there and got the other two guys, and we left. From what I understand, because of that incident with Tommy, they shipped Johnny out to California and told him, "Don't you ever bring your ass back here to New York!" That was one hairy situation that got out of hand before I knew it. I'm thankful for Tommy's help, because people have lost their lives over similar circumstances.

Another way the wise guys would get involved with recording artists is they would come to you and say, "You've got a decent record out there, and you're making good money. How much do you think you could make in a year?" And you'd say, "Well, I can make a hundred grand." Then they'd say, "Okay, what we want you to do is we want you to sign this contract, and we'll take over your management and handle all your booking." And then they'd open up a briefcase and there would be five-hundred thousand dollars in there. And they'd say, "We're gonna give you that. It's yours. And we'll book you. And whatever you make, we'll keep, because we already paid you five times more than what you say you can make."

So you would agree to it, because like in the Godfather, they'd make you an offer that you couldn't refuse. Then, they would book you at venues in Las Vegas, Atlantic City and the Copacabana in New York, where you'd make a ton of money every week, but they would collect all that money. And to make sure you didn't get any sticky fingers, they would send somebody on the road with you to make sure that you kept your end of the deal. You could only take a little money for your living expenses. Wherever you worked, they would take care of your hotel bill and your band, and they would give you a few dollars. But the bulk of the money went to them. So what they paid you for the year, they would be making in a week.

When you got paid, you were supposed to turn it over to the road manager or whoever was in charge of the money, and that guy would take it back to New York and give it to whoever he was supposed to hand it over to. But sometimes there would be an occasion where an artist might keep some of the money to put in his own pockets. When that happened, you'd get a knock on your door. These tough guys would take you and put you in a car, and they would drive you out somewhere in the desert outside of Vegas. They'd make you get down on your knees, and they'd cock that gun and put it right to your forehead. They would say, "Listen, cocksucker, you take another dime from me, and we'll leave your ass right here in the desert."

I know this sounds like a Hollywood production, but this stuff really happened. That's where the movies get it from! You'd really be lucky if they didn't harm you. Most of the time, they would just scare the hell out of you. But I'm sure that there were a few who pushed the envelope too far, and ended up in the desert permanently. You'd have to be careful. You couldn't make those kinds of deals if you weren't going to abide by whatever it was they said you were supposed to do.

The only way to get out from under something like that was if you were a big time entertainer on the level of Jackie Wilson or Sammy Davis, Jr. An entertainer of their caliber could find somebody higher up in the hierarchy, and make a new deal with them. They'd have to say, "I want you to manage me because these other guys are doing this, and these guys are doing that."

So this guy would then go to the other people and say, "Hey, I've got Jackie Wilson now," or "I've got Sammy Davis now. He don't owe you no more money." The new manager would be the entertainer's angel. But in reality, most of the time they were all in cahoots anyway. Everybody knew who was doing what to whom. The new manager would take over, then he would just take certain monies, and give the artist the bulk of the money. But they would always take their share. All this was the cost of doing business with the Mob.

When my wife Dedra got pregnant, Tommy asked me about him being the godfather, and his wife being the godmother. They both were staunch Catholics. I said, "Okay, let me talk to my wife." My wife said it was fine with her. We gave Carleen the middle name of Gaetana in honor of Tommy. So after we had the baby, they flew into Chicago. They stayed at the Holiday Inn on Lake Shore Drive. They went to Bergdorf Goodman and bought the baby a beautiful christening gown. We went to St. Ailbe's church. They stood up and went through the whole service. Then we had a little after-party, and my buddy E. Rodney Jones, the Chi-Lites, and some other people came by my house in Pill Hill.

Carleen had been born on my birthday in 1975. I was supposed to go to England on September 10th. I was talking to her in my wife's stomach. I said, "Listen, I've got to go to England. I'll be gone about a week. So don't come out 'til I get back!" I got back on the 17th or something like that. And then I told her, "Well, listen, there ain't but two more days. Just hold off and come out on the 19th, which is my birthday!" So sure enough, on the 19th, she said, "I'm out of here!" We got so many savings bonds from Tommy and Dorothy on Carleen's birthdays and at Christmas. They were just great godparents.

One day my doorbell rang, and these two white guys from the Internal Revenue Service were standing there, displaying their badges. They came in and laid some printouts in front of me. They said, "We're after him. They call him 'The Happy Killer.' You didn't know that?" I said, "No, I ain't never heard nothing like that!" They said, "Yeah, 'cause when he killed somebody, he used to laugh." I said, "Oh, no, you've got the wrong guy. This ain't the guy that I know."

They said, "We brought this to you because the statute of limitations is about to run out on him, and if you help us get him, then we're gonna help you in whatever problems you may have." They were trying to muscle me. So I told them, "You know what? I don't know what you're talking about." They said, "If you don't tell us what we want to know, we're going to look at your income tax every year!" I didn't tell them anything because I didn't know anything about the man they were looking for. So like they said, every

The Man Behind the Music

year, they audited my income tax because I wouldn't tell them what they wanted to know.

They asked me, "Is he co-management with you with the Chi-Lites, and this guy, and this guy, and this guy?" I said, "Yeah." And then he said, "Well, are there any times when you get paid that you get paid under the table, where you didn't have to pay taxes on it?" I said, "No, all of our money came through the booking agency. It's all written. It's all legit."

The IRS guy said, "Yeah, but I'm just saying, sometimes you can get it done another way, right?" I said, "No, I never did that. And I don't know who this Happy Killer is you're talking about either." After they left, I didn't call from my house, but I went out and called Tommy and I told him that they had come by my house. I told him exactly what I had told them. And he thanked me and everything. That's why when Tommy was called into the home of the "Old Man" one time and asked why he was standing up for this "nigger" (speaking of me) against someone that the "Old Man" was close to, Tommy told him, "He's the standup guy, not that one you're talking about!" We've been tight ever since.

Chapter 11

In 1975, the Chi-Lites were in the midst of a very successful tour in Europe. Being their manager, I flew over to London to see how things were going for myself. The concerts were very profitable, so the group was making a lot of money, which meant that I was making money, too. I flew over there several times a year to meet with my artists, and pick up my cut of cash for my management fees. I also had attorneys working on my behalf there – or as they called them in England, barristers – to handle my contracts and monitor my business interest. I really enjoyed going over to England. There was something about Europe that was altogether different and better than the United States. Over there, everything wasn't so much about race. They excepted you for who you were, and they particularly loved the Black entertainers. There were a lot of good times and cherished memories associated with my visits to Europe.

When I came back to Chicago after this particular European tour, my brother George, who was working for me at Brunswick, picked me up at the airport. At that time, I had a gold Rolls Royce that I would leave in his care. When he pulled up in my Rolls, I got in back and he handed me a newspaper with a headline that read, "Chicago Record Mogul Indicted." This hit me like a ton of bricks. Unbeknownst to me, while I was overseas, myself, along with Nat and several others, had all been indicted for allegedly selling Brunswick and Dakar records off the books and paying disc jockeys to play our records. I was completely blown away.

On June 24, federal charges were brought in Newark against a total of nineteen people in the record business. U.S. Attorney Jonathan Goldstein alleged illegal payments had been made by Brunswick to deejays and program directors across the country in return for radio airplay, an illegal practice commonly referred to as payola. There were also accusations of income tax evasion and mail fraud, as well. The two-year investigation was snaring some other big names in its net, handing down indictments on Kenny Gamble (the head of Philadelphia International Records) his partner Leon Huff, and Clive Davis (the former president of CBS Records and then-current head of the Arista label).

In all, six Brunswick executives and one of its business associates were all hit with the same indictment. Along with Nat and I, the defendants were Brunswick vice-president Peter Garris, the label's secretary Irving Wiegan, production manager Lee Shep, national promotion director Melvin Moore (who would be identified as the go-between for transmitting payola money to deejays and program directors), and Carmine DeNoia, a self-employed record salesman. It was alleged by the government that a sizable amount of Brunswick product was being sold off the books in exchange for cash and other merchandise, lowering the royalties paid to our performers and ultimately depriving the IRS of its share of tax revenues.

Obviously, I was very concerned. Why didn't I hear about this from somebody at Brunswick? To open up the newspapers and see it there was quite unsettling. So I called Nat and he told me I had to come to Newark for the arraignment. I flew into New Jersey, and that was the first time anyone informed me that I had to go get my picture taken and sign some court documents. To my astonishment, we had been indicted on twenty-four counts, and there was a maximum sentence of two years for each count. That means I was facing up to forty-eight years in a federal prison! This was a nightmare. I just couldn't rap my head around the idea that I could go to prison for alleged crimes that I had nothing to do with. I had no direct involvement with the operations at Brunswick's New York office. At first, Nat didn't seem to be too concerned. But once we started hearing all the charges that the prosecutors laid out, we knew we were standing in some tall weeds. The evidence stacked up against us like a deck of new cards. Evidence like: names, dates, amounts, witnesses and even wire taps. The feds' case was seemingly air tight. In all, more than seventeen-hundred documents would be presented to the jury, by a prosecutor who was hell bent on getting a guilty verdict.

Nat told me that I had been assigned an attorney that he had chosen to represent me at the trial – but this is where the plot thickens. My faithful friend Tommy came to me and said, "Hey, don't agree to let this guy represent you because he's gonna sell you out! I got word that they're going to use you as the scapegoat. They're going to fix it to make it look like you were the one who led all the black acts to the slaughterhouse!" Damn, they're going to try to hang me out to dry. I couldn't believe it! I was grateful for Tommy giving me the heads up, but it hurt me to my heart that Nat was in on this, too. So I was careful not to tip my hand, and I got another lawyer from Newark named Leonard Felzenberg. This lawyer was a real bulldog. He'd fool you because he came over as calm and collected, but he was something else.

The U.S. Attorney probably already knew that my co-defendants were positioning themselves to offer me up to be the fall guy. So his counter strategy was to get me to turn state's evidence against Nat and the other co-defendants. Even though I didn't like the fact that Nat and the others were trying to set me up, I wasn't about to have my singing debut be in a federal courtroom.

On January 14, 1976, Assistant U.S. Attorney Thomas Greelish made his opening statements before Judge Frederick Lacey and the jury. He argued that Brunswick had realized more than three-hundred thousand dollars in cash and another fifty grand in various merchandise. They cited numerous transactions with record stores and distributors that were kept off the books, particularly where merchandise like a new Cadillac sedan, color televisions, stereo components, washers, dryers, and sporting goods, were all given in exchange for product. The prosecutor characterized this alleged environment of greed and corruption as "Nat's candy store."

Edward Hurley, a former Brunswick sales executive who was the government's chief witness, testified that these under-the-table deals were made at below normal wholesale costs, with all transactions made on a cash basis. However, under cross-examination, Nat's attorney Peter Parcher impeached Hurley's credibility when he forced him to admit to having stolen twenty-two thousand dollars while he was a trusted employee of Brunswick.

    I was there in the courtroom almost two weeks before my name ever came up. Finally, I went to my lawyer, Felzenberg, and said, "What am I doing here? They haven't mentioned me in two weeks!" He said, "You're a stockholder. They'll get to you." Tommy's wife could have been a lawyer herself. She and Tommy raised two daughters and a son, and their two daughters did become lawyers. Every night when I'd get back to the hotel, I'd call Tommy's wife and explain to her what took place in court that day. She would delve into her law books and offer me some advice. Finally, she told me, "You know what, Carl? There's a certain law that says if they haven't come up with anything and they haven't mentioned your name, you can ask to be discharged from this trial." So I went back to my lawyer the next day, and I inquired about this particular law. He confirmed that what she had told me was correct.

    So I went to Nat and told him that I was thinking about using this technicality to try to get myself dismissed from the trial. Nat asked me not to invoke that rule because Melvin Moore and I were the only black defendants, and it would hurt the rest of them because the jurors were mostly black. Nat said, "If they discharge you, we won't stand a chance!" At first I couldn't believe it. The same ones who were going to throw me under the bus needed my presence to save their own asses. Man, the crap was getting so deep, I needed fishing boots. But despite how I felt, I told Felzenberg not to try that legal strategy.

    Sure enough, they eventually got to me. The prosecutor pointed out that most of the artists that were on the label were black, and that most of them were recruited by me. This was supposedly my link to the corruption. The government's assertion was, once the artist were signed, the company would begin embezzling money from them by selling records off the books, thereby cheating the artists out of their royalties. This was a bunch of crap. The fact was, I never wrote a check for Brunswick, and never put in an order for records. I didn't have anything whatsoever to do with the day-to-day operations of the New York office, other than to send them the product to be released by the label. At best, I visited the New York office maybe once or twice a year for meetings related to the release of my productions, or if one of my artists was headlining at the Apollo Theatre.

Carl H. Davis, Sr.

Seymour Greenspan, one of the owners of Summit Distributors in north suburban Skokie, Illinois testified that he bought thirty-four thousand dollars worth of Brunswick Records through me in 1971, making the checks out to me personally or Carl Davis Productions. But there was a plausible explanation for all that. What happened was, when we started building our own studio at 1449 S. Michigan, there was a rehearsal room back there, but there was no studio. So I told Nat that we ought to have our own studio. He said, "Carl, if that's what you want, go ahead and build it. And what I'll do is ship in so many records to our distributors, and then you go and pick up the checks or the cash and pay it to Bruce Swedien." Bruce, my longtime engineer, was building the studio for us. And that's how we financed building the studio, from reimbursements paid to us from distributors like Summit.

However, I didn't know that Brunswick wasn't recording those transactions. All I was told was, "Go pick up the checks from some of the distributors and pay it to Bruce." So that's what I did. Seymour got on the witness stand and tried to make it appear like I was getting money under the table. However, in cross examination my lawyer tore his butt up and made him testify to what really happened.

Lou Krefetz, the owner of a Baltimore record shop, testified that he'd also gotten reduced wholesale prices on Brunswick product for paying in cash. Krefetz made an important point: cash purchases of product weren't all that uncommon within the industry. Several other store owners and distributors detailed their various dealings with Brunswick, the prosecution attempting to single the label out as doing something underhanded, when in reality it was fairly widespread. Chicago distributor Willie Barney testified that he got 45s from me at a fourteen cent discount, then admitted he had a similar relationship with someone at New Jersey-based All Platinum Records. Willie was the one-stop distributor in Chicago, so if you needed any records to be distributed, you would sell them to Barney.

The prosecution brought Willie L. Williams, the former program director of WCMB in Inkster, Michigan from 1971 to 1973, to the stand to testify that he'd been handed several small cash payments between twenty-five and one hundred dollars as a thank-you gesture from Melvin Moore. At meetings at Detroit's St. Regis Hotel, E. Rodney Jones gave similar accounts that Moore had given him a total of two grand on a half-dozen occasions from 1971 to 1974 as a gesture of appreciation. Rodney also testified that he received round-trip plane tickets to L.A. when the Chi-Lites performed on The Flip Wilson Show. And Roosevelt "Rudy" Green of WJMO in Cleveland said under oath that Moore had given him an unspecified amount of money in 1972 along with the latest Brunswick release. All three swore that those negligible payments had not influenced whether they added Brunswick releases to their respective playlists.

In reality, payola really wasn't any big deal. You paid the disc jockeys and they played your records. We were the only ones ultimately taken to trial, but nearly everybody was doing the same thing. Those little cash transactions were generally for higher amounts than what was testified to at the trial. I think the disc jockeys pretty much got whatever they asked for. A sum like twenty-five dollars might have been a partial payment. Rodney and I were close friends, so I took him with me to Florida a couple of times. Another time, we went to Hawaii to play golf, and I paid for the airplane tickets for him and his lady, along with their hotel bill. But that was just normal procedure, because we were tight on a personal level.

Eugene Record of the Chi-Lites had pleaded guilty in early January to charges that he had failed to file U.S. income tax returns for 1974 despite earning more than one-hundred thousand dollars. The other members of the group had been charged as well. As their managers at one time, we kept their books for them, but as they got bigger, the Chi-Lites decided that they wanted to be responsible for their own books. And I didn't handle their record money.

Here's how our management fees were set up. If the Chi-Lites were booked through the Queens Booking Agency, Queens would take my twenty percent out of the deposit. If the gig was five thousand dollars, the promoter had to send twenty-five hundred of that as the deposit to Queens Booking. Queens took their percentage out as well as my twenty percent. Then they would give the Chi-Lites the balance. When the Chi-Lites played the engagement, they would get the remaining fifty percent.

I had hired some bookkeepers to keep up with all of their monies. We used to give them big envelopes to take on the road with them, and when they checked in or out of the hotel, they put all of their receipts inside this big envelope. At the end of the week, they'd mail it back to the office. Our bookkeeper kept track of everything, and then at the end of the year would file their taxes. But after awhile, they wanted to control their own finances, so I stayed out of their financial business. However, they got themselves into a world of trouble with the IRS and ended up getting indicted. I believe that's what gave the feds the leverage they needed to force them to testify against me and Nat at that trial.

On the stand, Eugene recounted the assault in Nat's office by Johnny Roberts, pointing out that I was there in the room as well. The inference they were trying to draw was that I was in on the muscle end of the business, which was completely untrue and Eugene knew that. However, the government's failure to produce Roberts as a witness didn't help their case any. As a result of what he'd done that day to Eugene as well as some other things, he was told to get lost. So they sent him out to the West Coast, where they made sure that he wasn't available to testify.

However, there was a lighter moment involving Marshall Thompson of the Chi-Lites when he came to the courtroom to testify. After they called Marshall to the witness stand, he came in there damn near dancing down the aisle on his way to the witness stand. A star struck young lady on the jury forgot all about juror protocol and asked Marshall for his autograph after he had testified. Although Marshall was seated near the jurors' box, he actually didn't hear her request. But this didn't stop the four-hour legal battle that resulted in her dismissal. Her courtroom indiscretion provided a needed distraction from a very taxing proceeding.

During the trial, the government referred to "Nat's candy store," the office where he allegedly stored some of those off-the-books records. When a lot of the distributors around the country were ready to do a return on their product, Nat would instead have them ship it out to my headquarters at 1449 S. Michigan because we had that big storeroom downstairs. This was old product that they couldn't sell anymore, so the distributors were returning the records for a credit. The U.S. Attorney tried to make it appear that this stock was my personal candy store, and Eugene agreed with that incorrect assessment.

I couldn't believe that Eugene would testify against me like that. Him being on that witness stand speaking out against me was like him stabbing me in the heart repeatedly with each disloyal word. He wounded me deeply. He didn't have to let them use him to try to bring me down. Besides, he never would have gotten in tax trouble in the first place had he continued to let my team handle the Chi-Lites' books. He put his own self in that position, and now he was going to side with the feds against me just to save his own butt. After all the things we have been through together, and all the years that we worked together. If it was someone else – one of the Mob guys or one of my competitors – it wouldn't have hurt so bad. But it came from someone who was my friend. That's what was killing me. Eugene could not even look me in the eye after he left the witness stand.

After the trial, he came out to my house. He actually had the audacity to ring my doorbell. It was obvious his conscious was eating him alive. To be honest, I didn't even want to open the door. He stood out there and apologized to me for about twenty minutes, telling me he was forced to do it because of what the U.S. Attorneys threatened to do to him. I didn't want to hear that crap. Excuses are like butt holes – everybody's got one and they all stink. So I just came out and told him, "Marshall was at the same trial, and he didn't turn coward and betray me! Marshall told all them jokers, 'Carl didn't have no candy store, and Carl never took any money from us!'"

Marshall got up there and told the truth, despite what the IRS was holding over his head. I guess Eugene was threatened with prison time, so he told the U.S. Attorneys anything they wanted to hear. He was really contrite and apologized until he was blue in the face, but it still took a long time for he and I to resolve our problems after he sold me out. However, as it is often said, time is the great healer. Eventually I would produce more hits on the Chi-Lites, but it was never quite the same between Eugene and I.

I didn't think the trial was going to last as long as it did, but it dragged on and on. After about four or five weeks, when I would leave the courthouse in the evening and walk to my car in the parking lot, a car would occasionally pull up in front of me carrying the forewoman of the jury, and she would look at me. You aren't supposed to have any contact with the jurors at all, but I couldn't help giving her a smile. Then I'd go to the hotel, and I'd come back the next day. I'd see her like that every once in a while. I would stay at the hotel Monday through Friday. On Friday evening, I'd catch a plane and come home. I'd stay home Saturday and Sunday, leave Chicago on Sunday night, and be back in Newark Monday morning. These were the longest weeks of my life.

I'm so glad that I didn't go with the attorney Nat was going to pick for me, because I feel that the results would have been much different. Part of my lawyer's defense strategy was not to call me to the witness stand, which would have opened me up to potentially damaging cross examination. Besides, why give the government a free shot at me, when the government had overwhelmingly failed to prove its case. A major fault in their prosecution theory was that they had no IRS representative to come forward to testify that Brunswick's business practices had defrauded the government of any taxes. They had claimed that I had access to the company checkbook and I had access to the sales at the pressing plant. So Felzenberg brought in the two secretaries from Brunswick, and they both testified that I came up there maybe once or twice a year, and that I had no access to either the bookkeeping or the checkbook. All I was in charge of was the music that had come out of Chicago. His witnesses actually testified in my favor.

Prior to the closing arguments from the lawyers, Judge Lacey dismissed fifteen of the fraud charges against us and gave DeNoia a directed verdict of acquittal, ruling that the case against him hadn't been proven. That took considerable weight off our heads. However, there was a conspiracy count and a sizable number of mail and wire fraud counts still hanging over our heads.

With seven weeks of testimony concluded, the judge turned the case over to the jury to render a verdict. The jury had a formidable job to do. They had to wade through seven weeks of testimony and arguments, not to mention the mistrial we almost had over the antics of the juror who wanted Marshall's autograph. I went back to the hotel. The jury deliberated three days. Day after agonizing day, I waited. Every time that phone would ring, I would jump out of my skin. It was truly nerve racking. My life and my freedom were in the hands of twelve strangers. For all these years, I had been so used to being in control of my own life – determining my own schedule, making my own decisions, being autonomous. But now it has all been reduced to one phone call and one verdict – guilty or not guilty. Then it happened; the phone rang. This time it wasn't my wife on the phone. It wasn't a supporting family member or friend. It wasn't room service or anybody else like that. They called because the jury had reached a verdict.

After receiving the call, I hurried down to the courthouse, but I was nervous as hell. When I stepped into the court room, it was different from all the other days that I had sat there before. There was a different atmosphere about, as only a day of reckoning can bring. All the other days were procedural, but not this day – this was it. This time, all us defendants were sitting

The Man Behind the Music

next to one another. I was the last one in the row.

The forewoman gave the verdict to Judge Lacey. He read it to himself and looked at us over the top of his glasses. In deafening silence, he then handed it back to her, and said, "Madam foreperson, what say you?"

"As to the defendant Tarnopol, on the charge of conspiracy, the defendant is found guilty. As to the charge of wire fraud, guilty." And when it came to the multiple mail fraud charges, Nat was found guilty on all twenty-two of those as well. Oh my God. Nat was like a Kamikaze plane shot out of the sky. He went down in flames.

Then she went down the line and read the verdicts in the same order we were seated. This one guilty, the next one guilty, guilty, guilty, guilty. They were slam dunking guilty verdicts like NBA basketball players slam dunk basketballs – one after the other. Then when it came to Shep and Wiegan, it got worse, because they were convicted on a 23rd fraud charge in addition to all the rest. However, there was a beacon of light because Melvin Moore was acquitted of all charges, and I was hoping that maybe that beacon of light might shine in my direction.

When I was coming up in school, having the last name of Davis always meant that I would be one of the first called, because the teachers always went by alphabetical order. It was the same way in the military. But here in the ominous New Jersey federal courtroom, I was the last person to have their verdict read. So by the time he got to me, I was a nervous wreck. When I reached into my jacket pocket to get my handkerchief to wipe the sweat that was running down my forehead, my hand was trembling. Then my lawyer whispered to me, "Do not sit close to the table. Back up a little bit," he suggested. So I complied, but when I did that, now I was close to the wall. How ironic that was, because now not only was my back figuratively against the wall, but now it was literally against the wall as well, which seemed like a bad omen.

The judge finally got to me. He said, "Madam foreperson, what say you?"

"As to the defendant Carl Davis…." And in an instant, my mind flashed back to weeks earlier when the foreperson passed me by in the courthouse parking lot and she looked at me – there was warmth in that brief second that our eyes met – and I responded with a smile. This brief second of fantastical flight gave way to the crushing weight of the most desperate moment of my life. She paused, then declared, "Not guilty on all counts."

When I heard the verdict, it was like the weight of this entire world was lifted off my shoulders and I just fell back in my chair. It was an indescribable feeling of relief and validation. I wanted to run over and hug the foreperson. From what I learned after the trial, ironically, there was a guy on the jury whose last name was Davis. During the deliberations, he apparently said, "I think Carl Davis was involved in it just as much as anybody else!" He turned out to be the one holdout that needed to be persuaded. However, after all was said and done, I was found not guilty.

Who knows, maybe the foreperson might have been the one who convinced the other jurors that I had nothing to do with it. She could have made him realize that he was wrong about me. After the trial, I introduced myself to her personally and thanked her and the other jurors, even though Judge Lacey admonished them for acquitting me. I couldn't believe it. Right when he was thanking them for their service, he said, "But I don't think you had the right decision on Davis." I was livid! I told my lawyer, "We ought to be able to sue him!" He said, "Carl, you've been acquitted, so just leave it alone and let's get out of here." I decided to take his advice.

Though U.S. Attorney Goldstein gloated over guilty verdicts at the post-trial press conference, it was a relatively short-lived victory. In the long run, nobody ended up going to jail anyway. Nat and his cronies stayed out of jail on bail while they filed appeals. Once they went back to court in 1977, a major part of their conviction was overturned by the U.S. Court of Appeals for the Third Circuit in Philadelphia. In June of 1978, during the retrial in Newark, Judge Lacey declared a mistrial for Garris and Wiegan. At that point, Assistant U.S. Attorney Kenneth Laptook asked Judge Lacey to dismiss all charges against Nat. Shep's case had already been severed from the rest.

As soon as the trial was over, I went back to Chicago and I told Nat that I wasn't going to stay here at Brunswick. After learning at the trial about the extent of corruption that permeated Brunswick Records, staying there was not something that I wanted do. If they stole from the artists, they were in all likelihood also stealing from me. So I let it be known that I wanted out of the company. Besides, with all the negative press that followed the indictments and the trial, all our names had been drug through the mud.

One day Nat called to summons me to New York for a meeting. I figured it was about my desire to leave the company, so I was on the plane the next day. After arriving at the headquarters office, when I got off the elevator, the receptionist warned me to be careful in there because there were some gangsters in Nat's office waiting for me. I shrugged my shoulders and I said, "What's that got to do with me?" Hell, I wasn't worried about nothing. So when I walked back there, sure enough, August Sims was sitting outside of the office. He was one of Jackie's longtime road managers, a bodyguard and an extremely tough customer himself. However, he too, warned me saying, "Be careful what you say, because they're looking to abuse you in there. They're gonna try to hurt you!"

I said, "For what?" I still couldn't believe that Nat would have me hurt. I gave him every successful record that he'd had in recent years, including nearly every artist he then had on the label. I had revitalized Jackie Wilson, who hadn't had a major hit in years prior to when I began producing him. Nat was like a brother to me. We had gone through a period together that was outstanding. I gave him hit record after hit record and made the company a major independent label.

A few years earlier, CBS had offered us fifteen-million dollars and a contract for five years to continue what we were doing, but Nat thought that wasn't enough and turned it down. I almost choked. I owned ten percent of the company at the time, so my share would have been a million and a half. Hell, I would have never had to work again. I could have comfortably retired and clipped coupons for the rest of my life.

But Nat said, "No, we're not going to sell the company. We're gonna buy the Yankees!" He was a Yankees fan. He loved them.

I responded, "What! The Yankees?" Has he lost his damn mind? I wasn't a happy camper about kissing off a million-and-a-half bucks. But I stood by him anyway, even when others (including me) thought he was crazy for that hair brain move. Hell, he was lucky they didn't whack his butt for turning down fifteen-million dollars and a deal with CBS.

After all of that, you can see why I thought I had done enough for him to protect me from any harm. Even if he was being pressured by outside tough guys who had infiltrated the company, he could have done more. I think they just had the hammer down on Nat. They were pressuring him into forcing me to stay. If I did split, they planned to do me a lot of harm.

So I went on in there. Sure enough, there were tough guys from the

New York family in there. One of them was a big old six-foot-four, three-hundred pound dude sitting there looking like he had a bad case of indigestion. Ironically, the guy with all the juice was the smallest person in the room. He was this teeny little guy who was there to represent "the old man." He was the one running the whole show. He said, "Your guy is with the same family as ours. We're all in this thing together. But I understand the problem is, you're talking about leaving the company, and if you leave and all the acts leave too, that puts Nat out of business. And since he brought your ass into this company, on his word he can have you chastised or whacked!"

They must have thought they were talking to Eugene Record, but I wasn't intimidated. I wasn't about to break down and start crying. So I said, "What are you talking about? First of all, Nat didn't bring me in nowhere. He wasn't responsible for me coming here. What was responsible for me coming here was I had a partner, a Jewish guy named Irv Nahan, and we started a booking agency in New York."

Then I explained to him what had happened with Irv and why we had to bring Gene Chandler over to the label and all of that. It was only after that incident that Nat and I started to discuss doing some other things, like me producing Jackie Wilson.

After they saw that I wasn't no punk, that big three-hundred pound corn-fed wop stood up and said, "Let me throw this nigger out the window!" That's when the little teeny guy told him, "Sit the fuck down and shut up!" Was I really afraid? Hell yeah! But if old Baby-Huey over there was going to try to throw me out that window, his big linguini eat'n ass was going with me. I was no light weight myself. I was at least two-hundred and twenty-five pounds and I used to keep myself in pretty good shape. So, little did he know, he would have had a fight on his hands.

But when it really came down to it, what really saved me that day was my friend Tommy, who was part of that same family and stood up for me. I left without being whacked because of Tommy and the truth. Tommy had told me to go to the meeting, tell the truth, and not worry about anybody. So I did. And when the guy said he'd throw me out the window, I just looked at him. I wanted to say, "Fuck you!" But I didn't say anything; I just gave Nat a defiant look.

Nat had been like my brother, so I couldn't imagine how this was happening. I asked, "How could you allow something like this to happen, after what I've done for you? I brought you all these hit records. Every hit record you got, I brought it!"

He said, "Yeah, but you know, you say you want to leave the company. If you leave the company, all those acts are gonna leave with you."

I replied, "The judge told every artist in there, 'As of this day, all of you are released from your contracts, because Brunswick was stealing from you.' It had nothing to do with me taking the acts from you. None of these artists are yours anymore, anyway."

During the trial, the judge had granted all of Brunswick's artists a release from the label, and I think that's what Nat was probably afraid of more than anything else. He would lose all of the artists that had been on Brunswick and Dakar, and he knew they would come with me.

Before the meeting was over, the little teeny guy came over to me and said, "Now you go back and you go see Tommy. You make sure you tell him that I didn't let this guy or nobody else abuse you, or nothing like that."

And that's exactly what Tommy told me in the beginning. He said, "You just tell the truth, and don't be intimidated by them." When the tough guys found out how I was brought into the company, they couldn't do anything to me. So all I had to do was get up and leave and go back home. I got a few of my personal things, got my coat and my hat, and left everything else. I didn't want no tapes, no nothing. I just got the hell out of there and didn't look back.

Back in Chicago, they installed a guy named Raymond Haley as Brunswick's new boss. I'd known him nearly all of my life, since he was a friend of my brother George when we were growing up. Raymond was selling insurance before he got into the record business. As a matter of fact, I bought a million-dollar policy from him. He was with New York Life or one of those other big companies. He tried to run Brunswick for awhile after I left, but the glory years were over.

Brunswick and Dakar struggled along into 1978. They ended up selling our old studio equipment to local songwriter Leo Graham, who worked closely with Tyrone Davis and had written and produced Tyrone's early 1976 hit "Turning Point" on Dakar just before Tyrone split for greener pastures at Columbia Records.

The final music and artists that left out of the doors of Brunswick and Dakar Records did so when a truck rolled up to 1449 S. Michigan, right there on the famed record row. There were no producers, promoters or A&R people present. But it was a team of movers who loaded the master tapes of all those fabulous artists and their golden sounds unto a truck bound for New York City. As the truck slowly pulled away down the street, the doors that were the gateway to fame for so many entertainers, seemingly took their final bow and then closed forever.

Chapter 12

Not long after the trial was over, I ended up going back to New Jersey. I wasn't really thrilled about going, but Tommy put a bug in my ear about another potentially very lucrative record deal on the horizon. Though he was short on the specifics, Tommy had already arranged a meeting with my music business lawyer, Leonard Felzenberg. After arriving in New Jersey, we met at Tommy's office and he told me that he worked out a nice deal with Artie Mogull, the president of United Artists Records. The deal called for me to deliver four or five albums, but the icing on the cake was they were going to give us an advance of one-hundred and twenty-five thousand dollars per album. That added up to somewhere in the neighborhood of six-hundred thousand bucks!

Since Brunswick was now closed down, we started Carl Davis Productions, Inc., and the new label called Chi-Sound was the subsidiary of the production company. Initially, I wanted to name this new label Chi-Town. However, the former manager of the Buckinghams, Carl Bonafede, claimed the rights to that name and he already had a single out on his Chi-Town label. So I renamed my label Chi-Sound. Everything was all done right after the trial was over. Tommy had gone out to California and negotiated with Artie

Mogull, while Felzenberg did all the paperwork to form the corporation.

Tommy and I flew out to California to finalize the deal. This deal was specifically tailored to place Chi-Sound under United Artists' distribution umbrella to issue our singles under their numbering system, as though they were actually on United Artists. This gave us the marketing and distribution muscle to make serious waves in the music industry. To accentuate the spirit of this new venture, I wanted to design a logo that captured the essence of the great city of Chicago. To do this, I included a silhouette rendering of the Chicago skyline and a twilight blue background encircled by rainbow-like colors. Nestled on the left of the big bold yellow and orange words "Chi Sound" was the black and white UA rendering of United Artists' logo.

I still remember getting that first check from United Artists for five-hundred and seventy-five thousand dollars, that was made out to Carl Davis Productions. There was still twenty-five thousand dollars left from the six-hundred. So then I received another check made out to me for the remaining twenty-five. The attorney who brokered the deal called his bank on our behalf and informed them that we would be coming to cash that check. So Tommy and I split it fifty-fifty.

Later on that day, we went out to Hollywood Race Track. That's where the harness racing known as the trotters raced. Ironically, a hard core guy like Tommy would only bet on the slower-paced trotters. As we were there sitting in the grandstand going over the thoroughbred stats on the racing form, somebody called out to Tommy from upstairs in the grandstand. Before he went to go to them, he said to me, "When the sixth race comes, put everything you have on this horse! Bet lights out!" Hell, that sounded good to him, but I never bet on a horse before in my life. He told me in no uncertain terms, "I don't care what you do on the other races, but on the sixth race, bet lights-out on this horse!" And I said, "Yeah, yeah, sure alright."

So I'm sitting through all the races, while he was up there with his rough looking buddies. Then when it got close to the sixth race, he whistled down to me, and I looked up there. He yelled, "This is the one!" I said, "Okay!" So I got up and I went to the window. I've got $12,500 in my pocket. And I thought, "I'm not about to put no damn money on this horse. The horse might break his leg or something." I think I put $500 on that horse, and I think Tommy might have bet $5000 on it. So now the race has started, and right from the beginning Tommy's pick led all the way to the finish line. I said, "Oh, my God, I should have put some more money on this damn horse!"

When Tommy came back down, he was elated and said, "Well, we got 'em, didn't we?" I said, "Ahhh, yeah." He said, "I got about $22,000. How much did you get?" I replied, "Ah, I got about $2500," which was just fine with me. He said, "You mean to tell me that's all you bet after I told you to bet lights-out on this horse?" I replied, "Tommy, that horse could have broken his leg going around that track."

When he found out that I only bet $500, Tommy was a little salty. He told me, "I ain't ever gonna give you another horse as long as I live!" And you know what, he never did. We've been friends for more than forty years now, and he's never given me another tip on a horse. A little later I was reading the newspaper, and that same horse was running somewhere in Philadelphia. I called him and said, "Tommy, I read where this horse is running in Philadelphia. Should I bet on it?" He hung up the phone on me. So I've never bet on another horse race since that day at Hollywood Race track.

By the time I had launched Chi-Sound, the once famous Record Row on South Michigan Avenue was no longer the local hub for thriving labels. So I set my sights on having our headquarters in a building at 20 E. Huron, not very far from where I'd worked for Columbia Records years earlier. In order to recreate that old studio magic – that distinctive Chicago sound that I had built a legendary reputation upon – it was necessary for me to reassemble some of my former staff. I called on my brother George, Gerri Harris, Jo Ann Brooks, Otis Leavill, and I even hired my daughter Pamela as the receptionist. With some key people in place, we got back to the business of making more hit records in the summer of 1976.

Almost right out of the gate, Chi-Sound had a couple of R&B chart records by Margie Alexander, "Worth A Whippin" and "Gotta Get A Hold On Me." Margie was born in rural Georgia and started out singing gospel before she went secular in Atlanta and joined Clarence Carter's revue in 1971. He produced her first two singles before we signed her. The girl was an excellent vocalist, and we sold a lot of records on her. Margie's first Chi-Sound hit broke in January of 1977, and the next month we had another R&B chart entry by an unlikely artist, who just so happened to walk right into becoming a vocalist – me.

Carl H. Davis, Sr.

The song was titled "Show Me the Way to Love," performed by Carl Davis & the Chi-town Orchestra. Its hypnotic intro cast a spell with its mystical eastern sitar-like sound, which evaporates into a funky yet mellow grove. As soon as the bass and horns kick in, I break in with these thought provoking lines: "life and love are ventures we set out on from day to day, never knowing how long either one of them is going to stay." Then beautiful harmonizing background vocals break in with the song's theme, singing, "Show me the way." This song is a Chi-Sound classic. And it flows like melting butter on a hot steamy biscuit. My arranger, Tom Tom Washington, and I sat down and banged out a classy melody that we felt could capture the essence of the now nostalgic Chi-Sound. Those first few poetic lines that I say in the beginning of the song, by today's standards would be considered as rapping.

In addition to their album (which featured lead singer Darryl Butler, his brother Morris, Samuel Beasley, Raymond Bennett, and Carl Winbush), they also had a couple of Chi-Sound 45s. Prior to Windy City's *Let Me Ride* album, they recorded two other singles for my Innovation II label. Innovation II was a label I launched along with my good friend E. Rodney Jones, even though he technically didn't have any actual ownership in the label. However, I did share part of the money that I received from this label's revenues. For this label, I made a deal with Warner Brothers and I got enough upfront money – around $125,000 – to give him twelve grand, which he took and bought a three-flat building with on Lake Shore Drive. Even though I was the sole owner of Innovation II, I always tried to find a way to look out for my friends.

Other artists on Innovation II included Wales Wallace, Simtec Simmons (he used to hang around the office so much that one of our producers took him in the studio and did something with him), the Lost Generation (a holdover from the Brunswick days), and Patti Drew (who had the hit "Tell Him" and whose only single for the label was a musical tribute to O.J. Simpson titled "The Mighty O.J.," who was still a pro football superstar in those days).

The Ebony Rhythm Funk Campaign was a nine member group from Indianapolis. Jay Johnson was one of the hottest disc-jockeys in Indianapolis and he was also their manager. They were a talented group, but their only R&B hit, "How's Your Wife (And My Kid)," came out on Innovation II in

1975. However, we wrapped up Innovation II because we were getting some static from Motown over the name of the label. Stevie Wonder had cut a huge album a couple of years earlier called *Innervisions*, and they didn't want any confusion between the two. After that snag with Motown, I closed down Innovation II.

The launch of Chi-Sound marked my happy studio reunion with Walter Jackson. When I left OKeh, Walter had to stay behind because he was still under contractual obligations to Columbia for another year or two. Walter had a handful of minor hits there without me, followed by one for Atlantic's Cotillion subsidiary. More recently, I'd done a Brunswick single on him, "It Doesn't Take Much," that made a brief appearance on the R&B charts in late 1973. However, none of those releases would compare with what we would do together at Chi-Sound.

We often recorded Walter at Paragon Studios, located across the street from our offices on Huron. Since Paragon was situated on the second floor, we would have to carry Walter up two flights of stairs because there were no elevators and he could only walk with the aid of braces and crutches. However, whatever he lacked in ambulation, he more than compensated for with his magnanimous personality and his magnificent voice. One of the songs on Walter's first Chi-Sound album in 1976, *Feeling Good*, was a smooth cover of Morris Albert's red-hot ballad "Feelings." This was my idea. I was looking for something classy like that for him, because I really wanted Walter to be a Nat King Cole kind of singer.

Morris Albert had "Feelings" out, and I just thought that Walter could do those kinds of songs – but only better. So we went after it and I put Riley Hampton on it to do the arrangement and orchestration. He did an excellent job, of course. I loved how Riley's arrangement leads in with those classic serenading violins and those soft guitar chords. Then Walter comes in with his golden baritone voice and simply says "Feelings…Nothing more than feelings." It was so good and it did well for Walter, breaking into the R&B Top Ten. We did something similar on his next album the following year, *I Want to Come Back as a Song*. This time Walter covered Peter Frampton's "Baby, I Love Your Way," and it became a sizable R&B hit as well. With Walter, you could try different things, because he could bring everything into the realm of what you were trying to do. Whether it was rock, pop, or whatever, when he put his style to it, it made the difference that only his voice could make. That same album had a remake of "It's All Over," the first hit I produced on Walter at OKeh, and that made some noise for him, too.

Each of Walter's first two Chi-Sound albums contained a song written by a pair of prolific British songwriters who were tearing up the rock world, although I'd first encountered one of them long before that. I used to go over to Europe on tour with Major Lance. A flamboyant keyboard player who was simply known by many as "Reggie" was backing many soul acts, including Major Lance. There was something fantastic about him even then. Every now and then in this business you'll work with greatness before it happens. It's recognizable, like certain people are already marked out to be music giants. When he was playing with Major, his creative genius seemed to ooze from his small frame. He used to always wear these tinted lens sun glasses, that later became his trademark. Though only few know him by his birth name, Reginald Dwight, the world certainly knows him by his stage name, Elton John. After I got to know him and his writing partner, Bernie Taupin, they gave me two songs for Walter, "Somebody Saved My Life Today" and "Sorry Seems To Be The Hardest Word." After Walter cut the songs, they sent me a plaque with the lead sheet on it, signed by both of them.

During this same period, Indianapolis was proving a hotbed of promising young talent for Chi-Sound. Jay Johnson brought us an up and coming act called Manchild. Jay was excited about these boys, and told us, "Man, I've got this group down here I'm managing. See if you can do something with this group." I didn't mind hearing his group because we needed Jay to play our other records there in Indianapolis. So we all jumped in a car and drove down to Indianapolis.

When we arrived at the radio station, Jay was on the air. After concluding his show, he took us over to a house and we met his guys. Their lead guitarist and saxophonist was named Reggie Griffin, who was related to the late jazz trumpeter Clifford Brown. Their lead singer and keyboardist, Chuckie Bush, was a tall, handsome looking guy, and "Flash" Ferrell did some of the lead vocals as well. However, the one who really stuck out was a teenaged guitarist named Kenny, who also sang backgrounds and wrote a lot of their material. The young man could write. He had some really good songs.

Sonny Sanders decided to produce them and took Manchild into the studio. We brought the group over, and then we went and had lunch while they recorded. Sonny did the production and wrote the charts. We did two albums on them, *Power and Love* in 1977 and *Feel the Phuff* the next year. *Power and Love* was a hit R&B album, and a single from it, "Especially For You," which Chuckie wrote, became a minor R&B hit in 1977. Ironically, I never knew what Feel the Phuff meant. That was their title.

During the 1980s, Kenny kept writing some great songs and had become successful with a group named Deele. From that point, he took off and became a big star under the stage name Babyface. He was so quiet back when he was with Manchild, and he seemed really appreciative of what we were trying to get done at the time. Years later, though, I went to a convention down in Atlanta, and by that time he was a big shot. He was "Babyface" then. The drummer from Manchild was still with him. So the drummer saw me, and he ran over and gave me a big bear hug, and we sat down and talked. Then Babyface came down the aisle. His band members called him "Face." One of them said, "Face! Carl Davis, man!" Babyface looked over at me, turned his head, and walked away. I didn't do anything wrong to him, and I never knew why I got the cold shoulder from him. So I never said anything else to him.

Chi-Sound only had two other female singers during the period when it was affiliated with United Artists. Della Reese was already a genuine mainstream star and had been for a long time. Her late '50s pop hits included "And That Reminds Me" and "Don't You Know." Somebody called me and asked me if I could do anything musically with her. I said we'd see. So I went out to Los Angeles to sit down with her and talk business. I had Walter Jackson out there then, too. He was getting ready to do Sammy Davis, Jr.'s television show.

I was up there in the hotel with Walter, Riley Hampton, and one of the Drifters. All of a sudden somebody knocked on the door. They opened it, and there stood Della Reese. She came into the room and asked, "Where's Carl Davis?" To my surprise, she wanted me to leave with her. So we left the hotel and went to Beverly Hills or wherever it was that she lived. She had a beautiful home. And she wanted me to spend the night. But that attempt to begin a relationship didn't work out. It was mutual. However, we still worked together. When she did come to Chicago, I took her over to the studio and Tom Tom did a gorgeous arrangement full of strings and horns

Carl H. Davis, Sr.

for her only Chi-Sound single, "Nothing But A True Love," which Della wrote herself. The project turned out to be really nice, but unfortunately nothing happened with it sales-wise. I imagine because it was not a commercial top-forty type song, it never did pick up any momentum. It was quite soulful, a bit jazzy, and really pretty, but just not commercially viable.

We also experimented with another female singer, a white girl named Madeline Peters, who just called herself Madeline on the record. She was married to Eddie Levine, the vice-president of promotions for United Artists. Eddie asked me to take her in the studio and do an album on her. The only thing that we put out was her single "Don't It Drive You Crazy." This too, never really made any noise.

In 1978, we brought another one of my favorite singers back on board. Gene Chandler hadn't had a hit since he left Mercury. His last single at Mercury was in 1972, "Yes I'm Ready (If I Don't Get To Go)." It was arranged by Tom Tom and co-written by Eugene Record. The Chi-Lites also cut it for Brunswick sometime earlier. As soon as he signed with Chi-Sound, he had a fresh hit with "Tomorrow I May Not Feel The Same."

That spring, Chi-Sound parted ways with United Artists. However, we put together a similar custom label deal that summer with 20th Century Records, where we would once again use the Chi-Sound logo. The catalyst for that deal was my old buddy Bunky Sheppard, their new vice president. He reached out to me once he found out that Chi-Sound's United Artists affiliation was going under, so I worked the deal through him. The current president of the National Academy of Recording Arts and Sciences (NARAS) was Neil Portnow. He was also the president of 20th Century Records.

Bunky had been a busy man since we ended our production partnership. He'd produced the Esquires' 1967 smash "Get On Up" in Chicago for his own Bunky label, then worked for several labels out on the Coast. At Motown, he'd worked under their president, Ewart Abner, his old pal from the Vee-Jay and Constellation days. Bunky deserved his success. He wasn't a great producer, but he was a great music man. He knew how to get your product exploited and played and promoted properly. All the disc jockeys liked him because he always took care of them. Some of Abner's largesse probably rubbed off on Bunky, too. Just to be in Abner's company was a delight. He was the kind of guy that whatever you wanted, you got it.

The Man Behind the Music

Bunky was the same old Bunky—you never saw him without his sunglasses on. It was great to work with him again. We had good times all the time. Bunky asked me to bring my acts over there, so naturally Walter and Gene were part of the package. Before the end of the year, we had Gene back on the high end of the R&B charts again with a dance tune called "Get Down." Dance music was quite a departure for both of us.

However, when Gene came back to Chi-Sound, he had recently had a drug pinch and caught a four year bit in the federal penitentiary. Fortunately, my lawyer got his sentence knocked down to a year. Since he only had a year or so to do, they sent him to the federal joint at Marion, Illinois, instead of Leavenworth or Oxford. Although Marion was a maximum security prison designed to take the place of Alcatraz, Gene wasn't in that part. The part he was housed in is what the Bureau of Prisons calls a camp. This was a lower level security facility for non-violent, white-collar crime inmates who had more freedom. Where he was housed was more like an Army barracks. While Gene was down there, my former banker was there doing a bit too, and he and Gene played tennis together during their recreation time.

Since, Marion was only three-hundred or so miles from Chicago, I would drive down there and take the track with me. We actually started working on "Get Down," there at the federal prison. But "Get Down" had to wait until Gene "got out." When we recorded "Get Down" initially, it was a no frills straightforward recording. However, Gus Redmond, Chi-Sound's ace promotion man, came up with a brilliant idea by suggesting that a guy named Rick Gianatos, who was a master engineer, should do a disco remix of the song. Though I really didn't have a preference for disco, the times and the music had changed, so I agreed. It turned out to be the right decision.

When all the remixing started, Rick was looping this, and dubbing that, and before you know it, he had completely re-engineered the entire song. I was completely amazed at what engineers were now able to do in the studio with all this new equipment. It really came out sounding good. The remixed version of "Get Down" turned into a marathon song that was more than eight minutes in length. Man, we put that thing out as a 12-incher and it ended up a smash near the end of the year, not just here in the states but over in Europe, too. Ironically, after Gene got released from prison, his break-out (no pun intended) disco hit was the biggest seller of his long and illustrious career.

Carl H. Davis, Sr.

During this same time, I had a brush with law enforcement too, but I was on the right side of the law. I was with the Cook County Sheriff's Department back then on a part-time basis. Ed Vrdolyak, who I was tight with, was my alderman. "Fast Eddie" was his nickname, but he was one of the most powerful members of Chicago's City Council. He had sent word on my behalf down to the sheriff's department to make me a sheriff. So they made me Inspector of Courts, and I had a gold badge and everything. Once Gene had been moved to a halfway house in Chicago, I worked out an agreement with the sheriff's department that as long as he was in my custody, I could take him out to L.A. to perform "Get Down" on Soul Train. We had fun doing it, and it was easy, because all the entertainers that appeared on Soul Train lip-synced anyway.

The following year on my label, Gene had a little more success with another disco tune, "When You're #1," and the mid-tempo R&B release "Does She Have A Friend?" However, neither one of these reached the same level of success as "Get Down."

Eugene Record had just rejoined the Chi-Lites when they signed with Chi-Sound. He had tried to go out and do some things on his own with Warner Brothers without much success. During the Brunswick court mess, when the government had claimed I was leading our black acts to the slaughterhouse, I kept telling people, "You know, when the deal goes down, you'll find out that if the acts are available, they'll all follow me to Chi-Sound!" And that's exactly what ended up happening. They knew that those charges weren't true. And they all knew that I was always fighting for my artists. Besides, the simple fact was that if the company bosses were stealing from them, they were stealing from me, too. If they were selling records off the books, then I didn't get my producer's share, neither did I get paid as a stockholder, nor did I get paid as a manager.

The judge had given everybody on Brunswick and Dakar an unconditional release, but after the thing settled down and I moved my headquarters over to 20 E. Huron, they all started coming back, one by one. I hired Eugene Record as one of my A&R guys, and Gene Chandler, too. Eugene and I weren't as close as we were before because he'd testified against me. Still, it was great to have the Chi-Lites on my label again. They all wanted to be back together. I think the only one who wasn't back was Creadel Jones. He'd gotten caught up with drugs. I don't know if he moved back to St.

The Man Behind the Music

Louis, but I caught him walking down the street one day. He was so high that he didn't know where he was. I felt so sorry for him that I had to take him home.

The Chi-Lites hit in 1980 with "Heavenly Body," and early the next year they did well with a remake of their Brunswick classic "Have You Seen Her." Both of those singles came from their first Chi-Sound album, *Heavenly Body*. Their encore LP *Me and You* had a couple more R&B chart entries on it, the title track and "Hot On A Thing (Called Love)," which turned out to be their biggest Chi-Sound seller in early 1982. That album also contained a remake of "Oh Girl." I felt these remakes were necessary to establish the fact that the Chi-Lites were now on the Chi-Sound label. We mostly did new songs, but when we did do the remake selections, we were careful to include fresh versions of the signature songs.

Although Curtis Mayfield had long ago left the group, the Impressions still had a name, so we signed them to Chi-Sound in 1979. Though they'd had plenty of hits during the mid 1970s for Curtis' Curtom label, they'd been floundering around for awhile before they came to me. A kid named Reggie Torian had taken over as their lead tenor. Sam Gooden and Fred Cash were still there from Curtis' days, and I had known them forever, since they sang on some of Major Lance's earliest OKeh hits. "For Your Precious Love," the Impressions' first hit a couple of decades earlier, had been fronted by Jerry Butler, but Sam could sing it just as well. So we went back and connected Chi-Sound with the Impressions legacy by recutting "For Your Precious Love" with Sam out front, and it made some chart noise in 1981. I cut two albums on them, *Come to My Party* and *Fan the Fire*.

Bunky had always been in love with the Dells. And with good reason: the veteran vocal quintet from south suburban Harvey, Illinois had been making hits since the mid '50s. They'd had an incredible eight-year run at Chess that ended in 1975, then they moved over to Mercury and had several more R&B hits there. But they'd just ended an unsuccessful stint at ABC Records when Bunky asked me if I would produce the Dells for 20th Century. I had been good friends with all of those guys for a long time, so I agreed and we went into the studio. I did two Chi-Sound albums on them, and I thought they were fantastic.

Eugene Record wrote the Dells' biggest Chi-Sound hit, 1980's "I Touched A Dream." To me, it was a classic song, and they did a beautiful

Carl H. Davis, Sr.

job with it. 20th Century sold a lot of copies of the tune, and it was the title track of their first album for the label, which also contained a lesser hit, "Passionate Breezes." On the Dells' second Chi-Sound LP, *Whatever Turns You On*, we redid their classic "Stay In My Corner" as the closing track. Once again, I tried to keep it as close as I could to the original version.

With all my old friends on Chi-Sound, it was like old times. We had a pretty decent following. I think everybody felt comfortable with me, and I felt comfortable with them. I wasn't looking for miracles, but I was looking to at least establish the label as one with hit product and hot acts. We tried again with Sydney Joe Qualls, releasing his 1979 album *So Sexy*, again produced by Sonny Sanders. We got some of the best blues writers that we could find for Qualls' album, including Prince Phillip Mitchell, and we sent Sonny down to Muscle Shoals, Alabama to cut some of the tracks. "I Don't Do This" has become a British favorite over the years, even though we didn't release it here as a single.

The only new name on our roster was Sugah, a female group that inaugurated the 20th Century hookup in '78 with their lone single, "Hung Up On The Feeling." I believe they belonged to the lead singer of the O'Jays, Eddie Levert, out of Cleveland. I gave him a $10,000 budget for that single on those girls.

In 1980, I moved Chi-Sound's headquarters into a four-story brownstone I had purchased at 8 East Chestnut on the Gold Coast, Chicago's ritziest neighborhood. At the time, I was probably the only Black in town who owned property on the Gold Coast. It was a townhouse that had caught fire and burned down. So I bought it for $170,000, and I got another hundred from the bank to rehab the place. I got William Brazley, an African-American architect friend of mine who had done some work for me at my house, to redesign the whole building.

They tore out everything and rebuilt it. I had a studio in the English basement. The first floor was a reception area with some offices. On the second floor, I had my offices. And on the third floor, I had an apartment with Japanese furniture. It was really a nice place. Carol Marin from WMAQ-TV came by and interviewed us on camera for their nightly newscast, and Black Enterprise magazine ran an article, too. William handled all the architectural duties for free in exchange for a favor. He was living out in the southern suburbs, and in order for him to get city business, he needed to have a Chicago

The Man Behind the Music

address. So I gave him the front office at 8 East Chestnut. In the front window, he put up a sign that said William E. Brazley & Associates, so that he had a ritzy location close to downtown. William would eventually expand his company into one of the Midwest's top black-owned architectural firms.

Marvin Davis, the owner of 20th Century Fox, stopped being enthused with the record end of the business. He just wanted the 20th Century movie tracks, along with the company's film and television divisions. So he dropped the record end of it. I got the label and all of my product back, and I went to M.S. Distributing here in Chicago. By this time, Milt Salstone, who had owned the company for so long, was not at the helm, but his son was. We made a deal with him to distribute the label as an independent. I think he gave us $25-30,000 and distribution, so we were doing alright. Then I went out to California and worked out some deals with some other companies to get national distribution.

Unfortunately, by 1982 there was a major shift in the music business and the disco invasion now dominated the market. Apart from Gene Chandler's "Get Down," our brand of soul was not really disco-oriented. The music business was changing and we were the dinosaurs, dying a slow death. Consequently, I paid a dear price for not being able to make the transition to the disco era. Since I had the responsibility of paying thirteen employees who all had families as did I, I tried to hold on and fight for the good music – at least, what I felt was the good music – to come back. But the train had already left the station. At that point, I was only fooling myself. If I would have made the decision to let my staff go and sold my company right then, I would have survived. But I kept everybody on the payroll and ended up losing the $500,000 or $600,000 I had left in the bank.

As a last ditch effort, we put 12-inch singles out on Gene Chandler and on the group Magnum Force. Their 1982 album *Share My Love* came out on my new Kelli-Arts label, named after my daughter. Led by brothers Rory and Ricky Sizemore, they were known as Seville when Otis first brought them to me. The title track had been a Kelli-Arts single the previous year and made some local noise without breaking nationally. I produced their album with Otis and Willie Henderson. But nothing could jump start Chi-Sound's vitality and vigor, and we lost too much momentum to turn around and catch up. Therefore, in 1984 we were forced to shut everything down.

Carl H. Davis, Sr.

Major Lance and I stayed pretty close after I stopped producing him. Although he had a few minor hits for Curtom, Playboy, and Osiris during the first half of the '70s, he apparently got pulled into another line of work shortly after he moved to Atlanta later in the decade. Since the music industry wasn't happening for Lance anymore, he tried to climb the slippery slope of drug trafficking and got arrested for dealing drugs. By this time, Major had become immersed in the dope game and apparently never broke the cardinal rule of using his own product, so he was able to make a living of it.

On one occasion, I had to travel to Atlanta. Once I arrived, I let Major know that I was in town. Later that night he picked me up and we went over to this spot where they had some pretty decent live entertainment. While we were there, I kept noticing Major getting up and walking over to a corner of the club, and some guy coming up to him and they would shake hands while exchanging something. Since I wasn't paying too much attention to it, it never dawned on me that Major was dealing. But when he came back over to the table, he gave me a thick roll of money and told me, "Just hold on to this for me." And I said, "I can sure use some of this." He said, "Oh yeah, you can use it all if you want! But for right now, I just need you to hold on to it for me." Well, I didn't have any problem with that. I got back to the hotel that night, and I counted it. It was like thirteen thousand dollars. Major never asked me for that money, and I ended up keeping it.

It had to be about six or seven weeks after I was down there that I heard he had gotten arrested, and then it dawned on me: damn, he was dealing that night we were at the club. Obviously the club was his spot. He must have been doing it for awhile, but I didn't know because that's not something that he cared to share with me. Maybe it was because he respected me so much, and didn't want me to know what he had resorted to for survival.

About a month later, I called his wife and told her, "I'm coming down there, and I want to go out and see him." She told me what the schedule of the visiting hours was. I rented a car and took a two-hour drive out to the prison. She and I spent a couple of hours with him down there. I asked him how it was. It was really a nice clean place. He didn't seem to be depressed or anything like that. Major was always upbeat. After Major was busted, he stayed in the joint from 1978 to sometime in 1981.

Why Major got involved with selling dope, I'll never know. Maybe he just got used to the fast money. When I was producing him, he was as hot

The Man Behind the Music

as a firecracker. I remember he used to be a boxer and he danced just like he was moving around the ring. His feet were mesmerizing, and his movements almost choreographed. He'd glide across that floor just like Jackie Wilson, and he would be spinning and splitting just like James Brown. He could do all that stuff very well. He was a consummate entertainer. He would always be clean and the women were always all over him. So that's how I cared to remember Major Lance, in the backdrop of those good old days. After he got out of jail, we stayed in touch and I never let his choices in life interfere with our friendship, so we remained good friends until 1994, when he died.

I'll never forget the night Walter Jackson passed away in 1983. My wife and I had attended a Jack & Jill event at Lewis University. Jack & Jill is an organization of mothers and children. It's one of the oldest black organizations in the country. We went out there to see a performance. It was close to midnight when we finally got home in Flossmoor, Illinois. Right as we were about to get into bed, the phone rang.

I don't know whether it was his bodyguard or his road manager on the phone, but he said, "Carl, something's wrong with Walter!"

"What do you mean something's wrong with him?" I replied.

He said, "Well, he's been drinking that 150-proof rum!"

At that time, Walter had moved down to 26th and Indiana.

I started yelling, "Mercy Hospital is right across the street. Why are you calling me? Hurry up and call the ambulance to get him to the emergency room quick!"

He started sounding very worried and he kept saying, "I don't know what to do."

I insisted, "Just hurry up and get somebody."

Then he said, "Hold on a minute!"

I could hear him shouting in the back ground, "Walter, Walter!"

Then there was a brief silence. He came back to the phone and said, "Carl, he's dead."

"What?" I shouted. I looked over at my wife and said, "He said Walter's dead."

I was just shocked. I told my wife, "Well, I'm going down there."

So I left, and I drove back into the city. By the time I got to the house, I guess he had called the hospital, and they had sent the ambulance over and took him away. When I got there, he wasn't there. But when Walter got to the hospital, they pronounced him dead. I sat around there for a couple of hours. His wife was there, even though they were separated at the time. They had adopted a set of twin boys, but they weren't there. I was so upset because it looked like the people who were there were only interested in his possessions. One guy wanted to take this, and one guy wanted to take that. I protested, "What are you doing?" So I was totally upset about it. By that time, I wasn't his manager anymore. I was just a really good friend. Sometimes when he couldn't pay his rent, the people at the real estate office used to call me, and I would send a check over there to cover his rent. I used to buy him a lot of stuff, like a boom box so he could listen to cassettes.

When Walter died, that was one of the saddest days of my life. He's still my favorite singer. I try to differentiate between my best artists, and who did the most for me, or who was a great singer. Walter was a great singer. Once I ran into Luther Vandross at a restaurant with Granny White, because Luther was on Columbia. Walter was alive then. And Luther told me, "Walter Jackson is my idol! He's what they call a singer's singer." I said, "He sure is."

I lost my right-hand man in 2002 when Otis Leavill passed away. That was really a shocker when he died. Otis went home one night, sat down in front of his TV, turned on his fan, and just died sitting in a chair. It hurt me to my heart. I was at work, and W.L. Lillard called me. He said, "Carl, our best friend is gone."

I said, "Who are you talking about?"

"Otis."

I said, "Don't tell me that."

"He's gone."

I couldn't even work anymore. I just got up and left, and drove over to his house. Sure enough, they had picked up the body, but his son and his wife were over there. This was also another great loss.

Many people who I have been associated with in my career in the music industry have passed away. I cannot mention all of them here. However, though many of us were friends, and sometimes even fierce competitors, as quiet as it's kept, we still had mutual respect for one another. The bottom line is in one way or another, we were all family and they too, are greatly missed.

Chapter 13

The downward economic spiral really started to take its toll. I managed to sell the building on Chestnut to the people who manufactured Pam. The owner's wife made it into a boutique, so at least I paid off both mortgages and had a few bucks left over. I still owned the house at 89th and Cornell, but the bank was trying to foreclose on me, because by that time I was defaulting on the mortgage. So instead of going through all the legal hassles, I just gave the house back to the bank.

Back in 1977, my family and I had moved from the first luxury house I had ever owned in Chicago's Pill Hill neighborhood, to an even larger home in south suburban Flossmoor. I had married Dedra, and she was pregnant with Carleen. I loved that beautiful place in Pill Hill, but it didn't have any backyard. None of the houses in that area did – it was typical urban living – lots of concrete, little grass. We even had a concrete fence. I still had my kids from my previous marriage living with me. There was nowhere for them to play in this little backyard. Dedra kept noticing that when our smaller children would play with my teenagers, they would play out in the street. My wife was very concerned about this, and rightfully so. She insisted that we move out to the suburbs, so we could have plenty of space for them

Carl H. Davis, Sr.

to play.

So we went house hunting out in Flossmoor, an upscale suburb about fifteen miles or so south of Chicago. We saw all of these beautiful rather large homes. There were plenty of trees, beautiful lawns, in a nice quiet environment that was perfect for raising children. As we were driving through various areas there, we pulled up into a cul-de-sac. We saw this house that was sitting way in the back. It was situated on 1.9 acres. There was a long U-drive that you pulled into. And what attracted us to it was that right there on the garage door was the pharmacist's mortar and pestle. My wife is a pharmacist. So we were immediately attracted to the house. While we were there, we went around to see the back yard. It was a nice size, with a wire fence encircling it. We had gotten the listing from the real estate company. After we looked at it, we scheduled an appointment to go inside. My wife and I loved it, so we bought the house.

After we moved in, I noticed that it was real soggy in areas of our back yard. So I consulted with a guy who owned a sports store in Lansing, who I had bought sports equipment from years earlier. I called him one day and asked him, "Can you build a tennis court?" He said he could. So I struck a deal with him to install a tennis court in my back yard. Then I also had them build a 10-foot fence around it, so that the balls wouldn't be flying all over everywhere. The village didn't want me to erect such a high fence, but I put it up anyway.

Right next to the tennis court, I had them put in a half-court basketball court. And we still had land left where our landscaper planted flowers. I had a little rock sidewalk that led to the tennis court. And inside, we had a little table with an umbrella. It was really nice. Then I put a black wood fence all the way around the property, except for where the driveway came in. That was open. I spent $35,000 on landscaping. We also had a swimming pool indoors, and I had them come out and drain the pool because there was a leak somewhere in there. They drained it out, fixed the leaky part, and repainted it. I had a sauna inside where the pool was. It was gorgeous. I was crazy about that house.

We lived in that house from 1977 to 1986, the year the Bears won the Super Bowl. I had six kids by then, and they all started graduating from high school. Carl Jr. graduated from high school, and he went to college in California. Then my daughter Pam, my oldest child, moved out and got an apartment with some of her girlfriends. Then Julio and Kelli went away to college. The only ones left were Jamie and Carleen. So with all my kids being gone, we didn't need such a big house anymore, so I sold it to a Jewish couple who lived in Flossmoor. I sold it to them for $280,000, which was a very reasonable price for that area, and was still able to make $100,000 in profit. With the proceeds from that sale, I bought a five-bedroom home that was considerably smaller, in Homewood, another nearby nice suburb.

By 1985, I was forced to sell my gold Rolls Royce. With the proceeds from that transaction, I went to the bank to pay off the money that I owed. The only tangible assets that I had left were approximately thirty masters that I was able to turn into a royalty producing vehicle that I could use as retirement income. After that, I tried to do some more recording, but it never amounted to much of anything. In the end, I was basically left with nothing.

After I closed down Chi-Sound, I did absolutely nothing for a considerable amount of time. Looking back at it, I was suffering from depression. I was burned out. It was like there was nothing left in me. The industry, the bankruptcy, and all the other legal problems that followed in the wake, just left me numb. My loved ones could see that emotionally, I was in a bad place.

One day my daughter told me that she had talked to a friend of hers at Lincoln Mall who was in charge of security there, and he wanted to give me a job. But then that's when the pride kicked in. I thought, "how would it look for 'the legendary Carl Davis, the man behind the music,' to be working security at a shopping mall?" But after awhile, the realities of having gone through bankruptcy and being broke really set in. The curve balls life throws at you will strike you out before you know it.

At one time I was living so high on the hog. I had money. I had prestige. But during this period of my life, I had little to show for it, except for that mountain of debt that was on my back. So it didn't take me too long to come to myself and realize that I could either sink or swim. Since giving up wasn't in my blood, I shook off all that self-loathing stuff and said, "What the hell. This is no time for a pity party" So I took that job!

It's funny, whenever we are in the midst of going through some serious changes in life, we think that everyone's talking about us, or that everybody knows. But most of the time, it ain't true. People are too busy dealing

Carl H. Davis, Sr.

with their own stuff to be worried about someone else's business. And I saw this for myself when I started working at Lincoln Mall in Matteson, Illinois. To my surprise, hardly anybody said anything to me. Yes, there was the occasional time when I would run into someone at the mall who knew me from the music world, and I knew they wanted to ask, "What in the world happened to you?" But they usually kept silent and didn't say a word.

Once I got back in the swing of working a regular 9 to 5, I had no problem with taking just about any other job that came along. I worked as a salesman selling janitorial products and I did other odd jobs as well. At that point, the only concern that I had was taking care of my family – not who recognized Carl Davis.

I had the job at the mall for a year. And then I accepted a position at Johnson Publishing Company as a salesman for a pair of radio stations that they owned, WJPC and WLNR. I was told that John Johnson, the company's owner, told the person who hired me to keep an eye on me, because I used to be a millionaire! I never really understood what he was concerned about. Maybe he thought I was going to do something desperate.

After Johnson Publishing, I went to work as a bank guard for Seaway Bank, whose president and majority stockholder, Jacoby Dickens, was a friend of mine back in the good days. He always treated me with respect and gave me a loan on a piece of property that I bought for my mom, who passed away in 1977. I was in the bank with my uniform on, wearing the star and the gun, and people would come in and know me. They'd be saying, "Carl?" But by this time, I had already reached the point that it didn't bother me anymore. I've been a hustler all my life. Before I started in the record business, I was hustling out there, going from one job to the next. I may not have had a bachelor's or master's degree from a prestigious university, but I earned my degree from the school of hard knocks, where I majored in survival.

There were a lot of times when I didn't think I was going to make it, until I experienced a spiritual awakening. One day I sat in my basement and began to talk with the Lord, just like I was talking to another person. I told Him how rough it was, going from being a millionaire to working as mall security, a bank guard and salesman for Johnson Publishing. And the Lord reminded me that He had not given up on me, so I shouldn't ever give up on myself. I still had all my kids and my wife, who all loved me very much. That's when it really hit me. If you have love in your life, love of family and

The Man Behind the Music

the love of God, you really have not been a failure, but are among the richest people alive.

It was then that I gave my life to the Lord. And slowly but surely, He turned my life around, and gave me a new perspective on life. With God and my family's help, I didn't end up like a lot of my artists, on drugs or dead. And there were many who couldn't handle the loss of status, and ended up committing suicide. God allowed me to experience His riches in my life, and good things started to happen to me and my family. Soon, I was blessed to receive monies from unexpected sources. Monies that had been held up over years of working in the business were now starting to come in. I began to rebuild my resources from master recordings that I had accumulated over the years. That's when I really started to learn that God lets us experience different things in life only to reveal His love and kindness.

It wasn't too terribly long before I attempted to dabble back in the music business once again. I developed my own little production company. I started doing radio commercials for the Cotton Club, a Chicago nightclub. I'd write the jingles and get the musicians, and we'd cut the spots – one minute, thirty seconds, all that. I also made commercials for a couple of local auto dealerships, utilizing the connections that I had cultivated over the years in the music industry. I had a pretty good little thing going for awhile doing that.

However, soon, that too, died out. But I got a call from a CD reissue company over in England, named Westside Records. They asked me about buying my Chi-Sound catalog, which I still owned, and I worked out a deal with them. It's possible if I had held out longer, I could have negotiated a more lucrative deal for myself. However, at that time, I didn't know the magnitude of the reissue market in foreign countries, especially Europe. So I made a deal with Westside for a couple hundred thousand dollars, and by me having little income at the time, that was a lot of money. Besides, like the old saying goes, "a bird in the hand is worth two in the bush." So I made the deal with them.

In 1987, the Dells came by. I had some equipment in my basement where I could actually record them, so we did some demos down there. Finally, I took them into Universal, and we did an album on them. Then I made a deal with a guy out of Jersey to distribute the record. I had to borrow some money from a bank to pay for the album. The guy in Jersey signed a note saying that he would be responsible for the payment to the bank. He sent them the first check and it bounced. Like a fool, I trusted him. But I should have known better because it was my name on that loan, not his. The bank wasn't interested in his note, they wanted their money from me, so I got stuck with that bill.

A friend of mine name Johnny Roberts was living out in California. So I asked him to do me a favor and go over there to get my masters back from this guy. He didn't have any trouble getting them. Those guys had the nerve to call me and say, "Man, you didn't have to do that!" I said, "Yeah, I did!" That incident killed the rest of the "maybe I could come back" stuff that was still in me.

After that sour note, I eventually went to work at O'Hare Airport as an airport representative for the Metropolitan Limousine Service. It was my job to pick up people getting off the plane. I'd be standing there at the gate holding a sign with your name on it. It was nothing really more than a glorified bellman. I'd help you go down to get your luggage. I had a radio and I'd call for your car and tell them what airport entrance to arrive at, and I'd put you in the limo. It got me back on my feet financially, with tips and all, to the point where I was making $35-40,000 a year. Then on top of that, I was receiving another $35-40,000 from royalties coming in from BMI and different places. So everything turned out alright after all. I ended up working for the limo service for eleven years, until I retired at the age of 72. By that time, my knees were in really bad shape and I had to have surgery on my right knee. So there could be no more long standing and all of that. It was time to hang up my hat and retire from working.

A few years ago, I was asked by several people, including Gus Redmond, to reactivate my Chi-Sound label, even though I haven't produced anything new myself. Other people wanted to release their product on my label because of its recognition, and I agreed. I have been able to interest some close friends to invest with me to pay for the pressing of products released on the reactivated Chi-Sound, friends such as Sterling, Earlyn, Kelli, Dedra, and Gene from Lexus. I have the utmost faith in a young man named Cornelius to actively run my company.

In the meantime, I had attempted to sue Brunswick Records for years because I owned ten percent of the stock in BRC and Brunswick Records, which would have been worth $1,500,000 if Nat had taken CBS up on its offer to purchase Brunswick for $15 million years earlier in our heyday. By now, I could have invested that $1.5 million and had no money worries for the rest of my life. But Nat turned the CBS offer down, and soon after the trial in Jersey, the company fell apart. Later on, Paul Tarnopol, Nat's son, took over Brunswick and revived it, reissuing the classic hits we produced on CD for a new generation of consumers.

I went to several lawyers asking for millions of dollars from Brunswick, and they all refused to accept the case because I didn't have my stock certificate. After years of trying, Paul eventually called me. We sat down and discussed the entire history of what happened, and how I was suffering financially. Paul said that he was under the impression that I sold my stock back. I said, "Well, if you've got the stock book, it's in there. You just look at it. You'll see that it was not a sale. It was used as collateral for a loan."

I had made a deal with Nat back when I was with Brunswick. My lawyer drew it all up, and I signed it. It gave the original stock certificate to Nat as collateral against a loan. When I had gone to divorce court, I was ordered to pay Beth $741 a month for child support and alimony. So Brunswick would automatically send her a check every month for $741, and in return for that, they held the stock certificate. If I had ever sold it to them, they would deduct whatever they had paid on the child support.

So I still had a copy of it, as well as a copy of the letters. On the back of the actual certificate was the total agreement. It stated that this was not a sale, it was just collateral for this loan. So all I ever had was a copy of the stock certificate, and my lawyer had possession of that. Nobody's ever been able to come up with that certificate, and I couldn't get my copy because my lawyer had died. Together, Paul and I worked out a fair agreement on what was owed me. We've forged a very good relationship, and he's been like a son to me ever since.

Chapter 14

When taking a retrospective look at one's life, one of the great questions that can be asked is "What has been the most important thing to you?" After you have scaled the highest peaks and traversed the valley depths, after you have endured the trials and tribulations of life, and weathered all the storms, what has been your motivation to carry on? Though these questions may not be found in the context of a simplistic response, I can start to answer by simply saying it's really all about love. It's all about the love of life, and the love that you have shared with others. For those of us who are rich in love have far greater wealth than all the money in the world.

Riches are deceiving. As quickly as they come, they go. A dollar bill never loved anyone, and yet people kill one another for a dollar. They sell their very souls for money. What a sad epitaph. As people with hearts and souls, we need to love and be loved. So looking back over my life, after all these years, I can truly say that love is the greatest thing that one could ever have. Love is better than a Grammy, better then a gold record, and better than a paycheck.

Love is so important. You've got to love people. You've got to love what you're doing. If you really want to do something well, no matter what

The Man Behind the Music

it is, you've got to really love it. True love always manifests itself when the pressure is on and when the chips are down. Everybody "loves you" when things are going well. Friends and people who say they love you come out of the woodworks in the good times. But what about when you are not at your best? When you have screwed up and have made serious mistakes, and are flat broke? Who really loves you will be shown then. It's not something you can just fake. True love demands that you be for real.

When I was in the recording studio, I was frank with my artists. If I thought they needed work or needed help or whatever it was, I would tell them, "You've got to get some more work done!" When you love someone, you tell them the truth. You respect them. So therefore, I was fair to my artists, and I always stood behind them. Since I was the type of person who invested my all into my artists, I didn't want just anybody. I had my choice of just about any artist that was out there, but I picked the ones that I felt I could be fully invested in. And at the core, love was the motivating factor because I loved what I was doing.

Let me tell you the difference between Berry Gordy and myself. First off, let me say that I respect Berry Gordy. Berry started off as a songwriter. He and his collaborators wrote some hits for Jackie Wilson first. Then when he started Motown, he was fortunate enough that he was able to go out and recruit Smokey Robinson, and Holland-Dozier-Holland, and all the other great writer-producers that he was eventually able to sign. Just like he was the head of Motown, I was the head of my record company, too. But here's the big difference: I went out and found all these great artists walking the streets, or somebody like my right-hand man Otis Leavill brought them in. I took them in the studio myself and produced their records. So it wasn't like somebody was handing me some artist that had already made it.

I would go out and get talented people like Sonny Sanders, Tom Tom Washington, and Johnny Pate to do the arrangements. And I would sit with them and hum every instrumental part that I heard and thought should be on a particular record. I'd tell them, "Well, I think you ought to take this guitar thing and put it with the horns," or "Take the piano and put it with the strings," or "Here's the beat I hear on this with the drums." I never got official credit for contributing to the actual arrangements, but somebody had to give directions on how these things were supposed to go. I was the one who put all of the ingredients together. I had to find the right artists with the right background, the right musicians, the right arranger, the right engineer. All of these things together, it was like a big melting pot. And to be honest, I never got the kind of credit I felt I should have gotten for what I accomplished. But I have no regrets.

That said, I don't have any regrets about my career in the music business. I wouldn't change it for anything in the world. I had a really good time. I was able to bring my kids along with me, and they were all able to share the joy of some of my successes that took place during that period of time. I raised eight kids in a pretty good lifestyle. As much as I cherished all that I was able to accomplish in the music industry, the most important thing to me was my children. I provided them a descent life, and I tried hard to set the best example that I could. I wasn't always perfect, but I always loved them, and they all know it.

All eight of my children still live in the Chicagoland area, and they're all doing well. I sent them to college and most of them graduated. A few went on to earn their master's degree. I'm very proud of them and some of the things that they've done for me. When things were really getting kind of rough and I was out at the airport banging the pavement and all that, they were the ones who sat me down and said, "Listen, you need to quit that job and just go home. Each one of us, we're going to do a certain thing for you each month." And that's what they did. So the kind of income that I was making out at the airport, my children made it up for me because they didn't want me out there pounding that pavement every day. That's love.

I also have thirteen grandkids, and four great-grandkids. Yes, I'm a great-grandfather! I noticed just the other day that one of my granddaughters had written to me on her Facebook page. She said, "You're the greatest grandad in the world!" That made me feel so good, because it was unsolicited. I have truly reaped the love that I sowed in them.

So I've never had any negative thoughts about the music industry, even though I may have been disappointed here and there. I never did get much in the way of Lifetime Achievement Awards or great recognition from my peers. But I still have no real regrets. I've enjoyed my entire life. Even the bad times, when the music business kind of died for me in 1983, and they were bringing in all that disco music. I was a music man, and disco was not my forte.

If you asked any one of the entertainers I produced over the years,

The Man Behind the Music

they knew that they could not come into Carl Davis' studio or office and fake it. They had to sing, because they knew I was right there on top of them, and I'd be the first one to tell them. I don't know if anybody else ever did this, but I would tell every artist that I had, "Do not come to the studio for a recording session with a lead sheet or a lyric sheet in your hand! You learn the song before you get here, so you can tell me a story. I don't want to hear you sing a song. I want you to tell me a story. And all of them – Jackie Wilson, Gene Chandler, and in particular Walter Jackson – appreciated that. You had to sing. Getting in there, picking up a piece of paper, and reading off of it just didn't happen in my studio.

By the time this book is published, I won't be living in Chicago's southern suburbs anymore. My wife's been after me to move to South Carolina for a while now. That's where she's from originally. We've got a house all picked out. Down there in the Carolinas, they've got what they call shag music. They still play all the records I produced back in the '60s and '70s, all my old Major Lance, Gene Chandler, Artistics and Tyrone Davis releases on OKeh, Constellation, Brunswick, and Dakar. As a matter of fact, in early 2011, Kraft Foods is playing one of Major Lance's hits, "Um Um Um Um Um Um," in one of their commercials. When I heard it, I looked up and said, "Major, they're still playin' our song."

Being down here in South Carolina now, I've had a couple of offers from people down here. They want me to help them out at some of their beach music nightclubs and put on some shows, or maybe work with some of their radio stations. I figure once I get settled down here, I'll probably get involved in something musical. There are more chapters waiting to be written in my story.

When I get my BMI royalty statement, you'd be amazed at all the countries that are playing my productions. They're spinning those classic hits in Japan and in Hong Kong. I'm probably bigger in England than I am over here. They had a big affair here recently at the Ambassador East Hotel. They had flown all these people over from Europe, and all they wanted was to see Carl Davis. Of course, they would have loved to have seen Curtis Mayfield, too, but he's not here anymore. Neither is Major. Fortunately, I still am, and it was great to meet them all.

A few years ago, I was inducted into The History Makers, a non-profit oral history archive located here on Chicago's near Southside that's

Carl H. Davis, Sr.

dedicated to preserving the history of successful African Americans in all fields of endeavor. Naturally, there are plenty of musical inductees – everyone from Nancy Wilson and Gloria Lynne to Kenny Gamble, Isaac Hayes, and my old friends in the Dells and Young-Holt Unlimited. Part of the induction process is you go to their offices at 19th and Michigan (right in the heart of the old Record Row), and they actually film you for three-and-a-half or four hours as you talk about your life from the time you were born up to the day you walk into that office. All in all, it's really a prestigious honor.

The night I was inducted, they held a black-tie event at the Palmer House, in downtown Chicago. My wife and I were there, and they honored me as well as Marshall Thompson of the Chi-Lites and Jerry Butler, among others. That was the night I met the future President of the United States, Barack Obama. He came by our table in the ballroom and shook everybody's hand as he introduced himself. Not just mine, but everybody's that was sitting at the table. I can't remember whether he was running for state senator or the U.S. Senate right then, but he was running for some Illinois office.

When Barack Obama made his announcement to run for the presidency, he did so from Springfield Illinois, the same place where President Abraham Lincoln made his announcement over one-hundred and forty years ago. As he walked up to the podium with his typical cool and confident swagger, amidst throngs of supporters and constituents, something heartwarming caught my attention. The melodic words to a classic Jackie Wilson song that I produced warmed the frigid temperature for those braving the cold that blustery February morning. Blaring out over the loud speakers I could hear "Your love keeps lifting me higher...higher and higher!" I was blown away. And I couldn't help thinking, "Wow, I wonder what made him pick that song?" I was really happy for him, and I supported him, even though I really didn't think America was ready for a black president.

A little more than a year later, as we all know, he won. On that unforgettable historic night in November 2008, Barack Hussein Obama was elected 45th President of the United States. When he and his family stepped out on the stage to address over two-hundred and fifty thousand hysterically jubilant supporters in Chicago's Grant Park, once again, they were playing "Higher and Higher." On that unforgettable magical night, I sat at home and watched the first African American become president – something that I

The Man Behind the Music

never thought I'd ever live to see. And they were playing my song at this defining moment in American history! This was the greatest validation that I could have ever received. I was so overcome with emotion that I broke down and cried. Out of all the songs that they could have played for that momentous occasion, they played one of my songs. I just wished Jackie was here to see it, too.

Later on, Maurice White, Granny White's son, called me and said, "You know, Carl, I was staying at the Hilton Hotel right across the street, and they must have played your song ten times!" At that point I just had to know. So I wrote President Obama a letter asking him what lead his campaign to chose that particular song. Unfortunately, I never received a reply. There is no way of knowing whether or not he even received my letter. So I guess I'll never know why that song was used. Though it's possible that someone on his staff may have been a Jackie Wilson fan, I would like to think that it was simply the most appropriate song that fit America's love affair with Barack Obama – the love that certainly lifted him "higher and higher" to the highest office of the land. After all, you can't get lifted much higher than the Chief Executive of the greatest nation on earth.

So at the end of the day, after all has been said and done, as I look back over my life, there have been many wonderful experiences with only a few regrets. Therefore, I can truly say that life has been good to me, and without the shadow of a doubt, I am fully persuaded that my living has not been in vain.

That's a wrap!

Letters From My Friends

The Man Behind the Music

Gene Chandler
Recording Artist / Producer / Executive

    I appreciate Carl Davis' efforts at the beginning of my career, in producing me, he and Bunky Sheppard, I appreciate his help as I moved on in my career. It was an experience, that had its ups and downs, but we always managed to come together to do what was necessary to make good music.

    As my producer, Carl and I worked well together. At that point in both of our careers, we were both relatively new to the business. However, there was one disagreement that I had with Carl that I'm actually glad he won. My concept of the "Duke of Earl" was that it would have strings behind it. That's what I was hearing and that's what I wanted. And I refused to record it without those strings. However, Carl was hearing a more solid beat as opposed to the softer melody that I was hearing. After going back and forth for a while, Carl got his way and we released Duke of Earl without the arrangement I insisted upon – and the rest is history.

    Carl was right, and "Duke of Earl" turned out to be a phenomenal hit that launched both of our careers. Therefore, I would have to say because he was the one who started me out, my career would not be what it is today, if it hadn't been for Carl Davis.

Gene Chandler

Carl H. Davis, Sr.

Jerry Butler
Recording Artist / Song Writer / Commissioner Cook County Illinois

Let me start by saying, when people talk about music, they often mention the Detroit or the Motown sound, or they mention the sound of Philadelphia, like Gamble and Huff. These cities all had a unique and distinctive sound. Then people will also ask me, Why doesn't Chicago have a sound? My immediate response to them is; Chicago does have a sound, as a matter of fact there is a multiplicity of sounds that have emanated out of Chicago.

For example, there was the sound of Curtis Mayfield, and the sound of Ramsey Lewis. There was the sound of jazz greats like Ahmad Jamal, and blues artists like Muddy Waters and Howling Wolf. There were also the sounds of what we know of today as gospel music, from greats like Thomas Dorsey and Mahalia Jackson, all of these sounds came out of the great city of Chicago.

However, one of the individuals that was response for making the *Chicago Sound*, all that it was and all that it could be, is my friend Carl Davis. Carl Davis brought to the table the sounds of Jackie Wilson, the sounds of Marshall and the Chi-Lites, the sound of the Duke himself, Gene Chandler. Try to imagine R&B without "the Duke of Earl." Indeed these were the sounds that came out of this great Windy City, and Carl Davis was one of the pioneering architects of Chicago's classic R&B music – some of the greatest music of our time.

Jerry Butler

The Man Behind the Music

Bruce Swedien

Five time, Grammy Award winning
Audio Engineer / Producer

2-17-11

I am honored to make some comments about my pal Carl Davis. Carl is one of the greatest producers that I have ever worked with, and I have worked with some of the absolute best. Carl is a friend and I think the world of him. I would love to have him as a brother – he means just that much to me. Carl has had a tremendous impact on the music industry. He was the driving force behind the *Chicago Sound*, and was behind some of the most talented artists in the industry. Whenever, you worked with Carl he made everyone feel like they were important. He knew how to listen, and he knew how to pull the absolute best out of his staff and artists. Though he was certainly about business, if you didn't have a ride to the train station Carl would stop what he was doing and give you one. He was just that kind of a guy. So far as my involvement with Carl, and what I think about him, the short story is "I love Carl Davis."

Bruce Swedien

Carl H. Davis, Sr.

Tom Tom Washington
Pianist / Arranger / Producer

Back in the 60's there were many independent producers in Chicago. There were also many arrangers, most notably Carl Davis. Carl used and had success with saxophonist Riley Hampton, and bassist Jonny Pate. I was introduced to Carl by Producers: Leo Austell and Bill "Bunky" Sheppard. However, it was actually producer and saxophonist Willie Henderson, who asked me to arrange *Turn Back the Hands of Time* for Tyrone "the wonder boy" Davis.

Carl thru Willis, got me to arrange tunes for Jackie Wilson as well as, Walter Jackson. Eugene Record also produced for Carl and primarily used Detroit's Sonny Sanders for arrangements, and started also calling me. Back then, Carl was producing for the Brunswick, Dakar and Atlantic/ Cotillion labels. After our music output began to grow, Carl expanded production by opening his own studio on Record Row. He eventually opened Chi-Sound records, where his office was on the famous "Gold Coast" at 20 East Hudson.

If I ever decide to write a book, the following is what I would put in a chapter of my novel. My view of Carl's legacy is that he opened up a lot of doors to the music industry in Chicago for young acts like: Magnum Force, Windy City, Davis Import, ERFC, The Lost Generation and Manchild, the group that "Baby Face" was in a member. Of course, these groups were just to name a few of the numerous groups and artist that Carl produced.

Doors were opened to younger musicians as well as for old. His range included utilizing jazz as well as classical musicians. He was multi-cultural inclusive change and non-bias in recording sessions with artist. The sounds that one may hear today, are samples of all that we did a long time ago. A lot of famous session musicians actually got their start from Carl Davis productions – that would include me. I recall he once allowed me to stand on his desk (that was Jack Daniels…Bunky's fault) and complain about some music. Quentin Joseph was with me – every bit of 190 pounds if we stood on the same scale. He listened to us and those who listened to him became successful.

Tom Tom

Tom Tom 84

Tom Tom MMLXXXIV

The Man Behind the Music

Sonny Sanders

Arranger / Writer / Producer

One of my many blessings is having a successful career in the recording industry for which I must give credit to several important people in my life. Berry Gordy gave me the opportunity of putting my first music notes to paper doing lead sheets for Motown, awakening my interest in writing music. Richard "Popcorn" Wiley asked me to write some of my first music arrangements for his recordings. Ed Wingate of Golden World Records, also gave me many opportunities to develop my arranging skills.

Back to my good friend until the day he passed away, "Popcorn" Wylie. In spite of my human frailties, he never spoke an unkind word to me or about me choosing instead to nurture and even promote my musical gifts and my career. Few people know that he was also responsible for my longest, most successful and still lucrative association with Chicago icon, Carl Davis. For a period of time, he pushed Carl to bring me from Detroit to Chicago and engage my services which Carl finally did after I had arranged The Reflections' "Just Like Romeo and Juliet" and Edwin Starr's "Agent Double O Soul" hit records.

Davis presented to me opportunities to further develop as well as expand my musical horizons not only as a music arranger, but as a songwriter and record producer, challenging me with an extensive variety of projects such as Louis Armstrong, Gene Chandler, Shirley Bassey, Jackie Wilson, Walter Jackson, The Chi-Lites, Young-Holt Trio and Mary Wells among others (I had previously worked with Mary at Motown; After her career had floundered, Carl signed her and breathed new life into her career). Carl racketed up quite an impressive track record of hit recordings. However, he also garnered much acclaim for production of many that didn't quite make the "hit" list. That's why I so proud to be in *the mix*!

Sonny Sanders

Carl H. Davis, Sr.

Neil Portnow
Producer / Record Label Executive
President / CEO,
The Recording Academy

"As a young man, having started early in my career as a musician, then record producer, and ultimately record label executive, I always was interested in learning about those who had come before – those that had the vision, judgment, and courage to find and develop the artists and creative talent at the very core of our industry and music itself. Carl Davis was one of those iconic individuals and someone I'd heard about over the years. With the very good fortune of being named President of the 20th Century Fox Record label in the 1980s, I found myself in the enviable position of meeting and ultimately working with Carl directly, as we signed a distribution arrangement with his Chi-Sound Records from Chicago.

Watching Carl's eye and ear for talent and repertoire, his attention to the "business" of promoting and marketing records, and his true love and respect for artists, I could see first-hand how and why he had earned his stature and place in our industry, and in the hearts of music fans everywhere. Gentle, yet firm and fair, Carl fought for his artists and for their success. And on a personal note, he introduced me to so many phenomenal and talented artists, songwriters, and producers – some of whom I still call friends today. I'm delighted that with the publication of this book, many more people will also get to share a glimpse of a true "record man" and the great music he has brought for all the world to enjoy."

-Neil Portnow

The Man Behind the Music

Gus Redmond
Promotions / Writer / Producer / Executive

Carl Davis was the first person that brought me into the music business. Carl was not only my boss, but he was also my best friend. Some of my fondest memories of working for Carl was as a road manger where I worked with artists like: Major Lance, Gene Chandler, Tyrone Davis, Otis Leavill, Lost Generations, and so many others. While working for Carl, I soon discovered that we were in the business of turning dreams into reality. This theme became so much of who I am today, that adopted "turning dreams into reality," as my motto. Whether it was in the role of being my friend, to being my boss and now even a being partner in the new Chi-Sound Records Label, Carl Davis stands at the forefront of those who contributed to my growth and success.

In retrospect, when I look at today's music, in contrast to the music of the 60' and 70's, sadly there is no comparison. Carl would have never allowed us to use the foul language or sing any lyrics that denigrated women or anything like that. Back then, we had standards of professionalism and pride and were sensitive to people and culture – something that you don't find with a lot of today's artists and music.

It is true that the times were different then; the music was different, society was different and race relations were strained. However, while making chart-topping hits, Carl was also charting the unknown waters of race relations in the music business. Whereas, black entertainers had long been on the frontlines of the fight for racial equality, Carl Davis was the first black A&R executive and record label president of a major record company. This was monumental. I'm not sure whether Carl knew at the time the historic significance of his accomplishments back then, but what I do know is that he was an example for all of us to follow. I am extremely grateful for all of what Carl Davis has meant to the music business in America and around the world. We who have laughed, cried, sang and danced to his music – through us the legend and his legacy – will always live on.

Gus Redmond

Carl H. Davis, Sr.

Phil Upchurch
R&B and Jazz
Guitarist / Bassist

Carl Davis is one of the greatest record men to this day-as proven by his body of work. He was a great person to work with. He wasn't a brain-picker like some producers. He knew what you had to offer when you showed up at one of his sessions. He was a master at picking all of the right elements to produce uncountable hit records. He had the Midas touch!

Phil Upchurch

Herb Kent
Broadcaster / Disc Jockey / Radio Host / Author
Radio Hall of Fame Inductee

I think that Carl Davis has meant everything to the music industry. During the 70's, he was really on a roll with artist like Tyrone Davis, Gene Chandler, the Chi-Lites and many others. Carl really understood his artists and what their music was all about. He was an all around man, and understood all the aspects of the record business. However, having said that, I also think that he has been underplayed, and never received the recognition that a producer of his caliber deserved. I truly believe that history will show, just how great a record producer Carl Davis really was.

Herb Kent

The Man Behind the Music

Otis Clay
R&B and Gospel recording artist

Carl Davis has meant a lot to me and my music career. Carl Davis was the first person to record me, in fact, the first time I had been in a studio to record as an artist, it was Carl Davis that did it. He was my first producer. For whatever I am as an artist, he was right there in the very beginning.

Most good producers, have their way of getting the best out of you and making you feel comfortable. However, some producers can be distracting. If they are a big celebrities themselves, it could be a little intimidating to work with them. However, a good producer can make you feel comfortable, that's where the real greatness lies – that was part of Carl's greatness. He knew how to bring the best out of you without overwhelming you.

He's always held a special spot in my heart, and I'm sure others will agree with me about this – Carl Davis is Chicago music as we know it today!

Otis Clay

Carl H. Davis, Sr.

Verdine White
Seven time Grammy Award winner
Bassist / Earth, Wind & Fire

Without question, Carl Davis was one of the greatest producers of our time. He produced some of the most unforgettable music of his era. As a young man coming up, I enjoyed a lot of the great music that emanated from Carl's studios. The production and song writing quality of his artists was quite impressive and served as an impetus for me to pursue my own musical interest. Another reason why I was drawn to his music is my brother Maurice played on many of Carl's recordings. Today, those same recordings are considered to be R&B classics.

Carl's contributions to the music industry are tremendous. They will never be forgotten. And I am so happy that in my life time that I was able to hear his work and cross paths with him. Whether they know it or not, a lot of the young artist today have benefited from Carl Davis' contributions, because his productions served as a foundation for much of today's contemporary music. So on the behalf of my brother Maurice and I, we are elated that Carl is finally receiving the recognition that has been long overdue. We wish him all the best.

Verdine White

The Man Behind the Music

George Davis
U.S. Air Force (Retired)
Publishing and Record Label Executive

First of all let me say that I don't know if I have enough accolades to describe how profound my brother's contributions to the music industry have been. As we were growing up together, I didn't realize exactly how talented my younger brother was. He was simply phenomenal. I was always amazed watching him in the studio producing. He had the extraordinary perception of his artist. Carl had ability to feel the artist and know exactly which direction to take them. So I was always astounded at his ability to produce just about any artist that he came in contact with.

As to his contribution to the music industry, Carl developed the Chicago Sound, however, he never received the credit that I feel he deserved. Many people picked up the Chicago Sound that my brother created, oftentimes without even knowing it. In that in that regard, Carl has had a huge impact to the music industry on a national and international scale.

Growing up as young kids, Carl was always the younger brother that you tried to keep out of trouble. There was always some excitement around my dear brother Carl. But one of the personality traits that Carl exhibited, even back then, was that he was trustworthy and supportive. Carl was very loyal. Whereas many of his delinquent behaviors he eventually grew out of, the loyalty stayed with him – the same loyalty that he gave to each of his artist. Therefore, I hope and pray that my brother receives the honor that he has earned and so desperately deserves. I love him dearly and I'm so thrilled that his story is finally being published.

George Davis

Carl H. Davis, Sr.

Johnny Pate
Bassist / Arranger / Producer

Carl and I go way back. Before Carl became the producer that made him famous, he use to be a record plugger for the distributors. He'd go around plugging records for various artist, taking them to radio stations and record stores, however, Carl had greater things in mind. After working his way up in the music business, eventually Carl became Vice President of Columbia Records.

At the time, I was playing bass, and I was also the copyist for Riley Hampton. I had seen Carl for many years around the record business, but one day I received a call from him and he told me that he had a record date coming up and he wanted to give me a shot at doing the arrangement. He said that he wanted to develop a different sound. Well it just so happened that that record date he was talking about was for Major Lance. The song, which turned out to be a big hit, was written by Curtis Mayfield, titled Monkey Time – and that was my introduction with working with Carl Davis. We had a ball, making some very great music.

There are so many great artist the Carl had a hand in putting on the map, but of course, Carl has always been one of those quiet guys that remained in the background. However, it was through working with Carl and Curtis Mayfield, that we created what other musicians and historians alike call, "the Chicago Sound."

After that first recording with Major Lance, I then began to work with Curtis Mayfield, the Impressions, and I did a lot over at ABC. Paramount Records then hired me as an in house producer, and that lead to further accomplishments that advanced my career. So Carl is really responsible for some of the success in my career. Had it not been for him, approaching me to do the recording dates with Major Lance, I probably wouldn't have gotten anywhere near the accomplishments that I did. Carl was right there and I have to give him credit for being a big part of my career and success.

Johnny Pate

Radio Stations That Broke Carl's Music During the 60's 70's and 80's

Carl H. Davis, Sr.

City, State	Radio Stations	Radio DJ's
Boston, MA	WILD AM	Steve Crumbley Elroy Smith
New York, NY	WWRL AM	Hal Jackson Rocky G. Vaughn Harper Frankie Crocker Sonny Taylor Jerry Boulding Hank Spann Jerry Bledsoe Jeff Troy
New York, NY	WNOR AM	Lee Michaels
New York, NY	WNBC AM	Walt Baby Love
Buffalo, NY	WUFO AM	Frankie Crocker Garry Byrd Jerry Bledsoe Ron Atkins
Buffalo, NY	WBLK AM	Ron Atkins
Newark, NJ	WNJR AM	Fred Mills
Philadelphia. PA	WDAS AM	Butterball Jimmy Bishop Georgie Woods Sonny Hopson
Philadelphia, PA	WHAT AM	Steve Turner Mary Mason Lady B.

The Man Behind the Music

City, State	Radio Stations	Radio DJ's
Pittsburg, PA	WAMO AM	Jeff Troy
		Ron Atkins
Baltimore, MD	WWIN AM	Al Jefferson
		Hot Rod
Baltimore, MD	WEBB AM	Tim Watts
		James Brown
		Fat Daddy
Washington, DC	WOL AM	Cathy Hughes
		Bobby Bennett
		Moon Man
		Jerry Boulding
		Sonny Jim Kelsey
Norfolk, VA	WHIH AM	Scotty Andrews
		Hotdog
		Paris Eley
		Bob Jackson
Norfolk, VA	WRAP AM	Jack Holmes
		Soul Ranger
Richmond, VA	WANT AM	Kirby Karlmichaels
Cleveland, OH	WJMO AM	Ed Wright
		Curtis Shaw
Cleveland, OH	WABQ AM	Ernest L. James
		J.L. Wright
Cincinnati, OH	WCIN AM	Bob Long
		James Alexander
Windsor, OR, Canada	CKLWAM	Walt Baby Love
Detroit, MI	WJLB AM	Al Perkins
		Jay Butler

Carl H. Davis, Sr.

City, State	Radio Stations	Radio DJ's
Detroit, MI	WCHB AM	Ernie Durham
		Fudi
Louisville, KY	WLOU AM	Bill Summers
Indianapolis, IN	WTLC AM	Spider Harrison
		Jay Johnson
Gary, IN	WYCA AM	Jim Raggs
Gary, IN	WLTH AM	Steve Brisker
Chicago, IL	WVON AM	E. Rodney Jones
		Pervis Spann
		Herb Kent
		Lucky Cordell
		Joe Cobb
		Butterball Crain
		Nausau Daddy
		Don Cornelius
		Walt Baby Love
		Dr. Cecil Hale
Chicago, IL	WJPC AM	Richard Steel
		Tom Joyner
		Kitty Nealey
		La Donna Tittle
		Sonny Taylor
Chicago, IL	WBMX FM	Ernest L. James
		Steve Harris
		Ray Cooper
		Steve Brisker
		La Donna Tittle
		James Alexander
		Bobby O'Jay
		Lee Michaels

The Man Behind the Music

City, State	Radio Stations	Radio DJ's
Chicago, IL	WBMX FM	Chilli Childs Marco Spoon Doug Banks Barry Mayo
Chicago Heights, IL	WMPP AM	Eddie Holland Ruben Hughes Big J.J.
Milwaukee, WI	WAWA AM	O.C. White Dr. Bop Larry O'Jay
Milwaukee, WI	WNOV AM	Jim Frasier Bill Kenner Ernie G.
St. Louis, MO	KATZ AM	Bernie Hayes Donnie Brooks Lee Michaels Johnny Jones Keith Adams
St. Louis, MO	KWK AM	Tony Gray
East St. Louis, IL	WESL AM	Jim Gates Doug Easton Jockenstein
Kansas, MO	KPRS AM	Dale Rice
Atlanta, GA	WAOK AM	Scotty Andrews Hank Spann Larry O'Jay
Atlanta, GA	WIGO AM	Burke Johnson Jack Gibson Ron Atkins

Carl H. Davis, Sr.

City, State	Radio Stations	Radio DJ's
Miami, FL	WEDR AM	Jerry Rushin
Charlotte, NC	WGIV AM	Chattie Hattie
Nashville, TN	WVOL AM	Gilly Baby
		Steve Crumbley
Memphis, TN	WDIA AM	Bobby O'Jay
Memphis, TN	WLOK AM	Melvin Jones
Jackson, MS	WOKJ AM	Poppa Rock
		Stan Branson
Jackson, MS	WMPR AM	Charles Evers
Greenville, MS	WBAD AM	Big Jock
Greenwood, MS	WGNL AM	Ruben Hughes
New Orleans, LA	WYLD AM	Gus Lewis
		Larry McKinley
		James Alexander
New Orleans, LA	WBOK AM	Ernie Singleton
Shreveport, LA	KOKA AM	Shelly Pope
		J.D. Black
Houston, TX	KYOK AM	Rick Roberts
		Wild Child
		Boogaloo George
		Walt Baby Love
Houston, TX	KCOH AM	Travis Garner
		Skipper Lee
		Wash Allen
		Paris Eley

The Man Behind the Music

City, State	Radio Stations	Radio DJ's
Beaumont, TX	KJET AM	Boy Brown
		Bonnie Brown
Oklahoma City, OK	KBYE AM	Ben Tipton
		Vernon Campbell
Los Angeles, CA	KGFJ AM	Alvin Wapple
		Walt Baby Love
Los Angeles, CA	KDAY AM	Jim Maddox
		Lee Michaels
		Doug Banks
		J.J. Johnson
		Jim Randolph
San Francisco, CA	KSOL AM	Bob Jones

List compiled by: Gus Redmond

Precious Moments In Time

The Man Behind the Music

Carl Davis, U.S. Air Force, 1951

Carl H. Davis, Sr.

Carl Davis   Bunky Sheppard   Gene Chandler

The Man Behind the Music

Carl Davis, Eugene Record, Tom Tom Washington,
Creadel Reed, Robert Lester (Squirrel), Marshall Thompson

Carl Davis in recording session with Della Reese

The Man Behind the Music

Carl Davis, Cholly Atkins, Gene Chandler, Don Cornelius

Carl H. Davis, Sr.

Left to right: Carl Davis, Marshall, Tommy, Squirrel, Eugene, E. Rodney Jones

The Man Behind the Music

Back Row: The Dells
Left to right: Eugene, Marshall, Squirrel, Creadel, Carl, Gene

Life To Legacy

Let us bring your story to life! With Life to Legacy, we offer the following publishing services: Manuscript development, editing and transcription services, cover design, copyright services, ISBN assignment and much more. You maintain control over your project because we are here to serve you.

Even if you do not have a manuscript, we can write your story for you from audio recordings and even legible handwritten documents. Let us bring you legacy to literary life!

Please visit our website:
www.Life2legacy.com, or call us at 877-267-7477.
You can also email us @ Life2legacybooks@att.net

www.ingramcontent.com/pod-product-compliance
Lightning Source LLC
Chambersburg PA
CBHW070742160426
43192CB00009B/1549